TO ASIA & LU

THANKS FOR ....
REMARKABLE SPIRIT
YOU'VE BROUGHT TO
THE CIRCLE!

THANK YOU

THANKS, AS WELL,
FOR ALL YOUR SUPPORT.
MAY WE SHAKE THE
TRAIL OFTEN ...
AND LET ME KNOW
IF YOU NEED SOME
COUNTERFEIT GREEN
CARDS!

11-15-15

TO ASM & LUKE,

THANKS FOR THE
TREMENDOUS SPEED/
PATIENCE BRINGING TO
THE CIRCLE.

THANKS, AS USUAL,
FOR ALL YOUR SUPPORT.
WILL WE BE SHARED THE
TRAIL? IF I NEED HELP
AND YOU NEED SOME
EXTRA CHARDS!

11-15-15

A Good Look Before Dark

A Warped Memoir

BRIAN PATRICK HIGGINS

Copyright © 2016 Brian Patrick Higgins

All rights reserved. No part of this book may be
reproduced in any form of by any means without
express written permission from
Brirish Publications:

P.O. Box 71
Alameda, CA 94501

tour@hillsandhops.com

ISBN-10: 1512396931

ISBN-13: 978-1512396935

Dedicated to members of
The Circle of Trust & Beer Hiking Club.
May our trails converge often.

"The world is big, and I want to get a good look at it before it gets dark."

John Muir (1838-1914)

CONTENTS

1	The Burning Bush	1
2	Into The Mystic	10
3	Fraternal Combustion	15
4	The Lackademic Journey of a Sub-Genius	29
5	Freeflailing	49
6	Worthless Yankee Currency	56
7	Now Coming to the Plate: Vengeance	67
8	Why Bars Close at 2 A.M.	76
9	Farewell, My Lovely	94
10	Texas Hexes	100
11	The Longest Day	115
12	Juror 5	137
13	The Dark Side of the Moan	159
14	The Prodigal and the Doppelgänger	172
15	Mountain Orgy	187
16	The Angel of Death	196

17	The Angel of Death Racks Up Frequent-Flier Miles	202
18	California's Seal of Self-Approval	210
19	The Circle Is Drawn	217
20	The Garden of Earthly Delights	226
21	The Marriage Poll	231
22	The Circle Inflates	240
23	Westward Ho	245
	Acknowledgments	251
	About the Warped Author	252

1

The Burning Bush

I was informed shortly after birth that I had two primary purposes on this planet: to root for THE Ohio State Buckeyes and to get to heaven (the good one, where the Catholics go).

The former came naturally to me; I still bleed Scarlet and Gray. I had to work at eternal salvation.

But given little choice, I decided to embrace the challenge. As soon as I was old enough to become an altar boy, I donned the uniform—a white surplice and black cassock that had lost none of its fashion sense since the Middle Ages—and went to work serving God through his branch office at St. Thomas the Apostle Catholic Church on the blighted corner of Fifth and Cassidy in Columbus, Ohio.

I rose quickly through the ranks. By fifth grade, I was training rookie altar boys how to genuflect without tripping over superfluous polyester and pointing out which angles on the raised altar provided the best views of the budding cleavages of our fairer classmates during Holy Communion. So when word came down that some nuances and accoutrements were being added to the litany of rituals that comprise the Mass, it was a foregone conclusion that I would be chosen for the trio of altar boys who would roll out the prototype at the noon service on Sunday.

Joining me on the A-Team were two of my classmates, Mark Solgeraud and Kermit Bradshaw. Mark was one of my best friends and a burgeoning psychopath who would matriculate to prison shortly after his 18th birthday for a point-blank murder. Kermit had long since rejected charm and chosen a militant attitude and a quick temper as his coping mechanism for being a black kid named Kermit.

Kermit's ambition was to become the first elementary school-aged member of the Black Panthers. One of the liquor stores in the area had a poster in the window depicting one of the seminal moments in the Black Power Movement: U.S. sprinters Tommie Smith and John Carlos raising a gloved fist on the medal stand at the 1968 Summer Olympics. Henceforth, Kermit would raise a fist to call attention to such white conspiracies as chalk on a blackboard or snow on our blacktop playground. He once got a week's detention for questioning the motives of a harried cafeteria worker who placed his mashed potatoes on top of his gravy.

On the Sunday that came to live in infamy at St. Thomas, Kermit, as always, was hogging the mirror in the church's basement. Possessed of a magnificent afro, it wasn't uncommon for him to spend 20 minutes staring at his own reflection while picking and oiling his foot-high mane into a perfectly symmetrical, Afro Sheen-ed work of art. As was his custom, Kermit finalized his ritual upstairs, in the vestibule mirror, as we were waiting in the wings for Mass to begin.

It was Monsignor Eastadt who finally convinced Kermit to line up for the procession that signaled the start of the service. The pews, as always, were packed. Monsignor Eastadt, whose age was the subject of a pool among the altar boys (the speculation ranged from 58 to 117), tended to drift so far astray of his script that he quickly lost sight of the shore. His M.O. was to stare blankly at his notes for a few seconds, contemplate the distance back to the harbor, then abruptly terminate the voyage with the magic words, "This is the Word of the Lord."

His aborted sermons were wildly popular among the men in the congregation, who could sleep in, hit the midday service and still get home in time for the kickoff of the Browns' or Bengals' game.

The good Monsignor huddled us together for a final run-through of the new playbook. He reminded us, among other details, that we would now be pausing in front of the altar and bowing to the bloodied, life-size figure of Dying Jesus on the crucifix behind the altar. Mark and I fixed our gazes on Kermit, who had been lukewarm on his bows during our practice sessions. Kermit didn't buy into the new program until one of the seminary students helping with the training pulled him aside and assured him that Jesus, being from Nazareth and all, wasn't really white.

Thus did we march off toward our sordid fate.

All went according to plan for about a minute, the time it took our little procession to parade up the main aisle of the church as the St. Thomas parishioners launched into the opening hymn. Mark was designated, largely on the basis of his bulk, to carry a freshly minted brass crucifix that could have doubled for a battering ram. Kermit and I shuffled in tandem two steps behind, trying to find our sea legs with our new apparatuses:

four-foot high candles.

Mark stopped on cue when he reached the foot of the altar. Kermit and I halted in perfect unison behind him. We cast a sideways glance at one another to coordinate our bow. As we had practiced in private minutes earlier, we silently mouthed a quick "one-two-three" and cast our heads forward.

Heeding the words of one of the altar boys who had reported back after nearly losing his balance with the new torch-candles at the Saturday evening Mass, I made my bow a cursory one.

Kermit, however, was feeling the heat of the eyeballs at his back. Word of our practice sessions had apparently filtered up the chain of command; as we were strolling around the side of the church to take our places for the opening procession, Monsignor Eastadt pulled Kermit aside and made it known, in no uncertain terms, that there was to be no malarkey with his bow— Caucasian Jesus or not.

So it was with great conviction that Kermit bent from the waist, like a peasant to an emperor.

What happened next passed into the great locomotive of legend at St. Thomas, interpreted and retold by the hundreds who were there to witness it, as well as the legions who later claimed to be.

Lifting my head from my own bow, I stole a glance in Kermit's direction to make sure we were in step for the final part of our processional journey onto the altar. I sensed a trick of the light, as if the midday sun and the stained-glass windows were conspiring to cast him in a blinding halo.

Kermit, whose suspicions already were elevated by the general lack of pigmentation among the assembled, began to panic when he saw my squint of confusion turn to wide-eyed shock. He had scarcely mouthed the words "What's wrong?" when I blurted out my assessment of the situation:

"Kermit! Your hair's on fire!"

"Say what?"

Coming to the quick realization that this critical exchange of information was being drowned in a sea of voices accompanying a pipe organ to "Praise God from Whom All Blessings Flow," I ratcheted it up a few decibels, making sure to over-enunciate every syllable.

"YOUR ... HAIR ... IS ... JESUS CHRIST!!"

I'm not sure whose face drained of color more quickly: Kermit, when he realized that I wouldn't dare utter such blasphemy with my mother camped in the second row of pews unless something had gone horribly awry; or me when I came to the quick realization that my mother was, indeed, camped in the second row of pews. Stout from childbearing with short dark hair and blue eyes that could throw laser beams, Mom considered the second row the ideal scouting location for detecting stifled yawning or other facial transgressions that might indicate I wasn't giving the Lord his due focus.

Fortunately for me, shrieks of horror from assorted female parishioners were now vying with the organ and the off-key singing to form a cacophony that transformed the mere six feet between us into an acoustical canyon. Nobody, including Kermit (who had merely read the reference to the Son of God on my lips) had heard a word I'd uttered. Moreover, I had tremendously understated the situation: Kermit's head was a bonfire.

I was trying to calculate if I had time to plant my ponderous candle in its base unit on the altar and return to Kermit's aid before his skull melted. That's when I was tossed aside by a set of bear-sized paws.

At 6-feet-5, Bill Hoffman was a gentle, pale, red-headed giant of a man whose eloquence made him a natural for delivering the readings of the Corinthians, Ephesians and other biblical gangs. The single women in the congregation could sometimes be seen applying lipstick when Mr. Hoffman patted down his hair, adjusted his tie and strode to the lectern at noon Mass.

On that Sunday, however, he was diverted from his mission. Dropping the parish's elephantine bible to the wooden floor with a crack that resonated above the din like a shotgun, Mr. Hoffman rushed to the rescue.

Kermit, who was quickly approaching Level Red on the panic scale despite being clueless of what all the fuss was about, heard the horrific thud of the Good Book and looked up to see the biggest, whitest man in the parish pushing me aside and bearing down on him with grim determination. The racial uprising about which Kermit had dreamed appeared to be upon him, and he, like General Custer at Little Big Horn, was coming to the quick realization that the enemy was holding all the cards.

Like General Custer, he would go down swinging. His first roundhouse glanced harmlessly off the thigh of Mr. Hoffman, who as far as Kermit could determine was trying to unscrew his neck and pound an opening in the top of his skull. Now Mr. Hoffman was nearly as befuddled as the altar boy that he was attempting to extinguish. Not only was Kermit not cooperating in stamping out the brushfire that he himself had set, but he was apparently trying to establish a perimeter, with his fists, to keep would-be firefighters clear of the scene.

The tighter Mr. Hoffman squeezed with his right

A GOOD LOOK BEFORE DARK

arm in an attempt to contain Kermit in a headlock while he risked the very skin on his left hand to beat out the flames, the more furious and desperate my classmate's resistance became. As the bible Mr. Hoffman had just discarded occasionally noted, few good deeds go unpunished.

With a front-row seat to our church's first-ever pyrotechnical cage match, I was a bit too captivated by the action to survey the general reaction of my fellow parishioners, an act of negligence I have long regretted. It would have been nice to place a few faces with the venue-inappropriate shrieks, profanities and high-decibel expressions of disbelief arising from the traumatized congregation.

Although time warped like a Salvador Dali painting, we later pieced together that it probably took Mr. Hoffman well under 30 seconds to contain the situation. As any smoke jumper knows, fires burn considerably faster uphill than down, and the forensic evidence would reveal that the flashpoint of the Great Kermit Fire of 1974 was six inches above his eyebrows.

From there, the flames raced upward, seeking the summit of Mount Afro Sheen. Kermit emerged from the headlock, ironically, whiter than Mr. Hoffman. But with the exception of his dignity and the previously well-tended garden atop his head, he was none the worse for wear. He would, however, forever have to wrestle with the conundrum that he had been rescued by The Man.

The show must go on, even after venturing to the outer limits of surreality. As Mark pointed out in the post-game debriefing that day, Jesus was probably pretty freaked out about the whole nails-through-the-extremities thing that he knew was coming, but he didn't call in sick on the original Good Friday. Kermit, too, was a gamer. After taking some time to regroup in the vestibule and figure out what the hell had just happened, he returned to the altar as Monsignor Eastadt was delivering the gospel.

Unfortunately, he timed his reappearance to coincide with the precise moment when Mark and I had finally pulled our acts together. With snot pouring from our noses and tears from our eyes, we spent the first 15 minutes of Mass desperately trying to repress the spasms of laughter that were racking our bodies. Even the stoic monsignor appeared to be unusually hard at work imploring the Lord to prevail over the demons that were tugging at the corners of his lips.

I was in hell, unable to look straight ahead for fear of re-establishing eye contact with Mark or the monsignor, but mortified by the thought of glancing in the direction of the congregation, where I was sure my mother was amassing evidence for what would be my ultimate come-uppance. But every time one of the parishioners gagged on a piece of afro—countless swatches of which were floating through the church like pollen—I surrendered more acreage in the battle for composure.

I was forcing myself to focus on a piece of chipped paint 10 feet above Monsignor Eastadt's chair when Kermit slipped in from the vestibule. His afro, previously as round as a basketball, resembled a field of corn stalks after the harvest.

It was too much for Mark, who let loose with a rollicking howl as a torrent of mucous escaped from his diaphragm.

With a genuine fear that my head would explode from the internalized pressure, I, too, lost my shit in front of the entire congregation.

As always, my parents were waiting for me after Mass near the grotto of St. Mary at the back entrance to the church.

My father, a jackhammer of a man who was approaching 40 and no longer sported a military haircut nor the physique of the ferocious football player he was in his youth, was ostensibly fiddling with his glasses after putting some distance between himself and my mother. It became apparent, upon closer inspection, that he simply didn't want any witnesses while he was doubled over in laughter. So much for my glimmer of hope that he would hustle us into the car in the name of the Cleveland Browns.

I had been bracing myself for the whirlwind of her wrath for the past half-hour, in part because the terror helped divert my attention from Kermit's head. Now that the moment was at hand, I simply lowered my head and took what I was pretty sure was going to be one of my last breaths.

"Lord help us all," Mom said, crossing herself as a closing salutation to the statue of the Blessed Mother, "but I'm pretty sure God himself was peeing his holy pants over that one."

2

Into the Mystic

Some of the most reliable fog in the United States is churned out on the western face of Montara Mountain, which rises from the California coast between the towns of Pacifica and Moss Beach, just south of San Francisco. There, in the cleavage of two ridges high above the nudists frolicking on the sands of Gray Whale Cove, ocean gusts collide with the land to put on a year-round spectacle for those who seek their thrills in the hills.

Starting at a thousand feet above sea level, Montara's windward slope is so dependable for producing swiftly moving, disconcertingly thick, trail-level clouds that we—the members of The Circle of Trust & Beer Hiking Club—have given this zone a nickname: The Fog Machine.

I have sought the fog since childhood, but there was precious little of it during my upbringing in suburban Columbus, Ohio. Except on Tuesdays during the summer.

That's when the DDT truck made its tour of our side of Bexley.

Missing the ice cream truck every now and then was no big deal, since it rolled through the neighborhood daily during the summers. But the Bug Sprayer, as it was known along Stanbery Avenue, only visited weekly. The kids on our street who failed to pay homage wore a badge of shame for the next seven days.

One block long with 11 modest houses on each side, Stanbery Avenue was protected by sight, but hardly by sound, from three tracks of freight trains which alternately ambled or blazed along the Bexley-Columbus border. A 20-foot-high hedgerow hid the trains, dozens per day, from gaze, but didn't prevent them from rattling every window in every house—Especially those of us on the north end of the street, where Delmar Avenue ran parallel to the tracks. The California earthquakes of my adulthood had nothing on the tremors I experienced daily in my boyhood.

The block was populated by first-time homeowners and their burgeoning families, and by retirees whose families we seldom saw. All seemed to enjoy the looks they drew when they spoke of their Bexley address, since the center of our suburb contained the Ohio governor's mansion and other castles of wealth along Parkview Avenue.

But on the northern fringes we dealt with seismic trains, cleanly delineating our border with a blighted area of Columbus, which my siblings and I walked through each morning en route to our Catholic education at St. Thomas the Apostle. Casting our lots wholly on the Bexley side, the lawns of our street were impeccably manicured (in part because I hustled cash by mowing and trimming them).

On Tuesday mornings during the summer, the mothers on Stanbery Avenue formed an alliance of sorts. The first to get wind of the approaching mobile merchant of death was responsible for sounding the alarm and making sure the kids on the street, from the sub-adolescents down to the recently toilet-trained, were assembled for the big event.

It was strictly a matter of style. Mrs. Cooper, the neighborhood divorcee, would race out to her front lawn, as often as not in a bathrobe, and launch into a tizzy that could be heard the length of the street. Mrs. Manring, who liked to chain-smoke in a lawn chair positioned close enough to the sidewalk to showcase her 38 Double-Ds to passers-by, would coolly direct the closest neighborhood kid to round up the troops, then go back to blowing smoke rings.

But we in the Higgins household rarely needed the prompt. Our mother had a preternatural instinct for sensing the vibration of the rumbling truck, whose mission was to thin the mosquito population by dispensing an aerosol cloud of industrial pesticide so dense that drivers following in its wake were obliged to turn on their lights and give the vehicle a berth the length of a football field.

"The Bug Sprayer is coming!" Mom would announce, sending me and my siblings scrambling like fire fighters. "It sounds like it's over on Northview Avenue!"

My brother, Patrick, tended toward panic if we weren't at the forefront of the group greeting the Bug Sprayer at the top of the street. "Alan Cooper just ran by!" he would screech, beseeching me to put an end to such anarchy.

A GOOD LOOK BEFORE DARK

"That damn Cooper kid," Mom typically grumbled in reply, using the occasion to list the various faults of Mr. Cooper, who remarried on the very day his divorce became final, or to comment on Alan's foul-mouthed mother, who used words like "hussy" and "slut" to describe the new Mrs. Cooper.

Urgency, however, did not permit indulgence in a favorite neighborhood event: kicking Alan Cooper's ass. The Bug Sprayer operated in a loose time window, and we often had only a minute or two to deploy to the south end of the street.

As the shiny metallic grill of the Bug Sprayer emerged from its own gaseous fog, we began our well-rehearsed choreography, parting into two groups to facilitate its passage as it turned left from Caroline Avenue. As the truck ambled by, the old black man behind the wheel flashed a toothless grin, waved and shouted his weekly warning above the roar of the machinery: "You kids don't come too close now, y'all hear!"

That was our cue: The race was on.

The object was to be the closest competitor to the fire hydrant-sized nozzle at the rear of the truck when it completed its obliteration of the insects of Stanbery and turned left onto Delmar Avenue.

As in car racing or distance running, there was some strategy to drafting off your competitors. So we pursued in shifts, rotating in and out of the prime position at the center of the bumper as our burning eyes and rebelling lungs dictated.

It wasn't so much a contest of speed. All but the youngest kids could keep pace with the truck as it puttered the length of the street. But once you fell behind to shake off temporary blindness or a bloody nose, it was tough to catch up. Due to limited visibility, the victors weren't always clear cut. On one controversial occasion, the handicapped kid across the street mysteriously materialized near the finish line when the lethal fog dissipated. The consensus was that he was already positioned there when the race began.

Like any endurance event, it was a matter of persistent training. In my younger summers, I sometimes caved in to the urge to spray down my blistering face with Mrs. Pastor's hose when the pack reached the midpoint of the street. By the time I was 8 or 9, however, I was consistently claiming victory— even when I was handicapped by the weight of my infant brother, Dennis, who Mom insisted that I keep within arm's length while she was watching *As The World Turns.*

The fun was over before my adolescence, by which time dichlorodiphenyltrichloroethane (DDT) had been banned in the U.S, and then internationally, condemned as poison to the planet. But it did its job in Bexley, where mosquitoes plummeted from the skies like rain. As did a lot of other winged creatures.

Thus was my taste for fog—and a general lack of common sense—ingrained for life.

3

Fraternal Combustion

I met my best friend while urinating. I was a freshman at DePaul University in Chicago and nature was calling. There were just two urinals at Players Bar, a popular watering hole located on the outskirts of the urban campus that catered to the under-age crowd. I was occupying one of them when a bespectacled, angular-faced guy whose curly blonde hair was already beginning to thin sidled up to the other.

"Hi Brian," he said. I turned to the right and vaguely recognized him from the dorms. But I couldn't place his name, if I'd ever known it. Seeing as how we were practically standing shoulder-to-shoulder, the moment was shaping up as highly awkward.

That's when I felt the warm spray on my hand. My toilet mate, trying to steady himself while delivering opening salutations, misfired to the left for a second or two after releasing the dam of Old Style Beer his liver had recently processed.

Glancing downward would normally have been a major violation of urinal protocol. But the rules, in this case, were clearly suspended. As I recoiled to survey the damage, the Luck of the Irish—which is often accompanied by getting pissed upon—strolled into the room. My bathroom mate was wearing a black jacket from his job at a furniture rental store. Emblazoned in bold white lettering on his left breast was his name.

"Oh, hey … Scott," I replied. "Your aim's a little bit off."

Thus began a relationship that has endured for over three decades.

It very well could have ended before it started, because that very night Scott and I found ourselves vying for the same bleached blonde. She wound up walking home with me, but Scott was the real winner, because she turned out to be multi-layered, from her pancake makeup to her girdle, the only woman of my generation I've ever known to wear one. It proved to be a chastity belt. So it was that Scott and I instantly established the ties that bind heterosexual males: competitiveness and sexual frustration.

Our friendship has been cemented by the usual guy stuff, including athletic competition, road trips, a night in jail, hiking Death Valley in July and not getting laid by the same women.

But it also survived an acid test far beyond any conflict of interest with a co-ed.

It all began with a sophomoric stunt at the end of my freshman year, when I lit a bottle rocket under the door of an uptight resident advisor who patrolled my dormitory hallway with a decidedly anti-marijuana prejudice. My conspirator was a senior named Vic Juska whose brother had presented him with a small arsenal of fireworks for graduation. There were no witnesses to our prank and there would have been no consequences, but for my partner in crime bragging openly to our fellow dorm residents, many of whom had been dissuaded from bong-a-thons under the R.A.'s regime.

Justice was swift. On Monday morning, less than 48 hours after we lit the wick, Vic and I received our dormitory eviction notices, simple notes tacked to the dorm bulletin board and signed by the Rev. Thomas Croak, one of DePaul's deans. Vic read his notice, laughed and wished me luck as he headed out the door, degree and luggage in hand, to begin the drive back to his native Florida with his parents.

For me, however, this was problematic. I had a job unloading trucks at UPS that paid over $10 an hour, three times the minimum wage in 1981, and had planned to spend the summer (not to mention my sophomore year) in the dorms. I suddenly found myself homeless.

It got more humbling in a hurry. Having won re-election to a lowly position in DePaul's student government shortly before my pyrotechnic stunt, I was obliged to spend several days at a student leadership conference in Shelbyville, 200 miles from campus. Shelbyville is located on the Axis of Boredom that runs between Chicago and St. Louis in a cornfield known as "Illinois." Joining me and my fellow politicos on the bus trip was the newly appointed faculty advisor to the student government—the Rev. Thomas Croak.

In Chicago, I was a microscopic bug in the world of political scandal. But in Shelbyville, I wore my shame like a scarlet letter ("A" for Attempted Arson). At one point, each of us was obliged to draw a piece of paper from a hat filled with all sorts of leadership qualities that Father Croak imagined we would possess. We then had to address the group with an impromptu three-minute speech on the subject. When my turn came, I stepped forward with trepidation. I was, understandably, wary of pieces of paper filled out by Father Croak. In the awkward moment that may have soured me on politics for life, I found myself lecturing on the importance of … envelope please … moral integrity.

Back in Chicago, I found temporary residence in what seemed like an ideal abode: the apartment above Players Bar. But it came with an ultra-creepy 32-year-old undergrad roommate. In retrospect, I have no excuse for failing to foresee "ultra-creepy" and "32-year-old undergrad" merging at some point.

When that arrangement abruptly ended in a gentleman's disagreement (fistfight) at the outset of my sophomore year, I found myself back in the market for housing when housing was most competitive. During the month it took me to find another apartment, I transformed my cavernous, metallic black 1973 Ford Galaxy into a part-time bed and full-time storage locker for my furniture, appliances, bedding and VCR porn tapes. That didn't squelch anyone's enthusiasm for riding in the car, however, because the big attraction was up front: an over-zealous pump that ejaculated windshield fluid up to two lanes to the right. It provided endless enjoyment at red lights. But it was the only thing on the car that was mechanically sound.

The vehicle burned oil so relentlessly that I had to keep a case of Quaker State in the trunk, where it competed for space with the brake fluid that I bought in bulk. Stopping was hazardous enough when there was plenty of room to spare, but in city traffic my friends learned to master a maneuver that we called

"The Flintstone," whereby we would slide our feet out of our respective doors to halt the car once it had slowed to below 7 m.p.h. or so. I once chose to steer the car gently into a tree rather than rear-end a Mercedes at a traffic light.

It was Scott who gave this smoldering box of liability its nickname: "The Ghetto Cruiser." It was a tribute to the boat-sized vehicle in which a pimp was ushered about the seedier parts of town on a popular TV show. Like my Galaxy, the pimp's car had opera windows, oval portholes cut into the vinyl roofing that gave a VIP mystique to anyone riding in the back seat (when the back seat wasn't crammed with my worldly belongings, that is).

On the long night that will forever live in the annals of our friendship (and nearly ended it), Scott and I ventured into the suburbs, forced to squeeze together in my front seat, much of which had been annexed to stash the personal belongings to which I needed quick access during my vagabond stage: clothes, toiletries and porn magazines.

Our intramural football teammate, Kip, was performing with his band at Haymaker's, a locally renowned nightclub in Mount Prospect. Kip's girlfriend lived in our dorm, but he had another arrangement altogether in Oak Park, a suburb 12 miles west of DePaul's campus.

Although his qualifications seemed suspect to me (he was a black guy from Toronto), Kip contended that he was part of a foreign exchange program. The female half of the alleged couple who "hosted" Kip in a well-appointed home was an attractive 40-something who wore revealing clothing and encouraged us to drink liberally from her home bar. The man of the house was never around; his very existence became the source of scandalous debate among our circle of friends.

Kip's Sunday night show at Haymaker's ended after midnight, by which point Scott was stressing about his Monday morning class load. He was enrolled in DePaul's business school so, unlike Kip and I, he took class attendance seriously. But he was also buzzed, so he conceded to the majority when our three-man vote to continue the party at Kip's cougar shack in Oak Park yielded a 66.7 percent affirmative result.

With plenty of room in Kip's van, there was no need for Scott to straddle the dirty pile of clothes in my front seat. We were all set to launch when I made the fateful suggestion that Scott and I switch places. After all, I reasoned, I was the only member of the trio who didn't know the suburbs (Scott grew up in nearby Palatine) and if I got separated from the van, I'd be lost. I didn't feel it necessary to mention my real motivation: the bag of weed in Kip's glove department.

To my surprise, Scott agreed—on the condition that we travel on surface streets the entire 20 miles. For some reason, he didn't trust the Ghetto Cruiser at highway speeds. I tossed Scott my keys, he and Kip verbally mapped out a route, and off we went.

Kip and I were soon ablaze and listening to a tape of that night's performance. Things were good in the front of our mini-convoy.

On the back end, however, Scott was learning that oil and brake fluid weren't the Ghetto Cruiser's only addictions. It also guzzled gasoline. That's assuming there was gasoline in the tank to be guzzled, which, I had neglected to mention, there wasn't. Somewhere along the 12-mile stretch of Harlem Avenue that we were traversing southward, Scott hit the accelerator and got no response. After some desperation foot-pumping, he began honking the horn and flashing the headlights to let us know that he was in trouble. Although Harlem Avenue is a major thoroughfare, it was practically barren in the wee hours of Monday morning. So Scott was beyond baffled when Kip's van just kept going, the taillights disappearing into the night.

In our defense, Kip and I were embroiled in a lengthy debate. As a purple haze filled the van, Kip had the audacity to put forth the theory that plain M&Ms were superior to the ones with peanuts. That devolved into a Doritos vs. Pringles debate. By the time we decided to settle the whole matter by stopping at Circle K, there were no longer any cars in the rear-view mirror.

Somewhere in the darkness astern, Scott used the last burst of petroleum to steer the Ghetto Cruiser onto a side street and abandon her where she died, vowing to see my head impaled on a stick.

We'll never know exactly how much time passed before Kip and I came to agreement that there was nobody following us. But shortly thereafter we nobly tabled our overwhelming urge for munchies, did a U-turn and headed back the way we came on Harlem Avenue.

A few minutes later, a small cluster of cars zipped by us headed in the other direction. But with our facilities as dull as butter knives, we couldn't decide if we had seen a Ford Galaxy or a Ford LTD, if it had been black or green, or if Pop Tarts should be heated or eaten straight from the wrapper. We circled back.

Six U-turns later, we came to two conclusions: Doing U-turns on Harlem Avenue was getting us no closer to Scott (or the Hostess Twinkies in the cupboard at Kip's place); and doing U-turns on Harlem Avenue was a bad strategy for getting through the suburbs, especially since one of us was black and both of us were stoned.

Which was just as well, since Scott—having cycled through bewilderment, rage and detoxification—had begun zigzagging his way in a generally eastward direction toward his dorm room, roughly 15 miles away.

In the era of cell phones, the whole mess could have been avoided. But the technology of the times didn't explain the pain that Scott put himself through that night, for he passed dozens of pay phones. He wasn't at a loss for friends who would have picked him up, even at that hour. But that wasn't the way Scott rolled. Raised in less than ideal conditions, he adopted a fierce independent streak early on. His determination served him well in coming years, when he was forced to live a Spartan existence after foregoing a business career to pursue a pilot's life. But that night, he may have been determined to outpace some abandonment issues.

So onward he marched, until at last he dropped from exhaustion in somebody's front yard, abandoning hope of attending his Monday morning classes.

Meanwhile, in Oak Park, we were raiding the refrigerator, pantry and bar at Kip's place. We called Scott's dorm room, but the phone went unanswered. Many beers later, we still hadn't come up with a strategy for finding our friend. But we did, at long last, come to a truce on M&Ms, with Kip acknowledging that the peanut variety was an appropriate choice for Cubs games and other sporting events, while I conceded the plain ones might be better for entertaining chicks.

A dozen or so miles away, Scott's camp-on-a-stranger's-lawn plans were being scuttled by the Chicago Police Department. The cop who rousted him decided he was harmless, but flatly denied his request for a lift to campus. The conversation, as Scott recalled, went something like this:

Cop: "I can't give you a ride, sir. But I have marked your location."

Scott: "What does that mean?"

Cop: "I've marked your location—in case something happens."

Scott: "What would happen?"

Cop: "An incident."

Scott: "You mean like someone killing me in one of the shitty neighborhoods between here and DePaul?"

Cop: "Any kind of incident."

Scott: "Thanks."

Cop: "Be safe, Mr. Davis."

Long about then, Kip, having satiated all his other appetites, decided to drive to the dorms, where he could ponder the matter further while having sex with his girlfriend. It was all the same to me, since my residence-on-wheels had—along with Scott—vanished in the night.

It was past 5 a.m. when we arrived at Clifton Hall. The first shards of light were beginning to break up the night sky over Lake Michigan, a mile east of DePaul's campus in Chicago's Lincoln Park. Predictably, the security guard was asleep. Kip used his girlfriend's key to gain entry to the women's side of the dorm, and I used the one I had never surrendered to get into the men's side.

I knocked softly on the door of Room 420. Nick Maucieri, who lived in Room 422, walked through the common bathroom and groggily answered the door. I recounted the events of the night. Nick reported that he had been studying all night and hadn't heard the phone in either room ring.

It had been a long day, beginning with our flag-football victory on Sunday morning in Waveland Park, along the lake. Scott, Kip and I were teammates on "DOA," a collection of incorrigibles which, to the surprise of all of us, advanced to DePaul's intramural championship game that fall. I was fried and homeless. Nick started to prepare for class, but invited me to hang out. While he was showering, I collapsed into Scott's bed, grimy and stinking of beer, weed … and the roast beef and pastrami hoagie that Kip and I purchased at Mr. Submarine on our way to the dorms. I fell into a deep slumber.

I dreamed of giant M&M's, the kind that would later become a staple of their TV ad campaigns.

I was ripped from sleep by a shrill, curse-laden, demonic diatribe, as if a drill sergeant and a longshoreman had inhabited the same body and were competing to kill me by myocardial infarction as I regained consciousness. I raised my hand in front of my face, partially out of self-defense and partially as shelter from the spittle that was pelting me from forehead to neck. I ventured one eye open and cautiously peeked through my own fingers. It took me a few seconds to recognize the beet-red, pulsing head discharging all the sputum and profanity.

Soaked in sweat and itching from the herbicide that covered the lawn on which he had attempted to spend the night, Scott had staggered down the dorm hallway to complete his 15-mile trek from the Ghetto Cruiser. Anticipating a hot shower and a glorious slumber, he unlocked his room, only to discover the object of the rage he'd been cultivating for the past six or seven hours snoring contentedly in his bed.

The Guinness Book of Records doesn't track the most uses of the word "motherfucker" in a 10-minute period, but I'm pretty sure the standard was established that morning. There were quite a few "assholes" thrown in as well, and I distinctly remember the whole soliloquy being tied together with various death threats. On several occasions, Scott demanded a detailed recounting of the events that led us to desert him on Harlem Avenue. But each time I opened my mouth, he immediately rebutted with a variation of "Fuck your explanations, you motherfucking asshole."

Like the Ghetto Cruiser, Scott's tank abruptly ran dry. Exhausted, he at last revealed the approximate location of the car and produced the keys from a pocketful of change. I wisely decided to pass up the opportunity to explain the correlation between loose change and pay phones. I grabbed the keys and made a hasty exit.

A few weeks later, I found an abode that was the envy of all my friends: the garden apartment of an upscale brownstone owned by a successful young couple, directly at the midpoint of the four-block walk from the dorms to Players Bar. I reclaimed the back seat of the Ghetto Cruiser, which held as many as five passengers once devoid of furniture.

When you pee standing up, there's a time limit on grudges. Scott held out for a couple of days, after which I called an impromptu meeting of my DOA teammates at Player's Bar to discuss a trick play that I wanted to insert into our upcoming game. With the clank of our beer mugs, the incident was put to rest. That is, except for the 2,742 times Scott has retold the story over the years, adding a bit more drama and suffering with each account, until it was easy enough to imagine that he had dragged a crucifix and been scourged by Romans for the entire route.

Against all odds, both the friendship and The Ghetto Cruiser survived my transfer to Southern Illinois University in Carbondale to pursue the journalism degree that DePaul didn't offer. Scott and I found excuses, most of them alcohol-related, to make the 350-mile journey between the two schools. After my junior year, when it was clear that SIU would be demanding tuition each and every semester, I took a year off to get my financial act together. I relocated to Chicago and performed the mind-numbing task of proofreading documents at the downtown Chicago law firm where Barack and Michele Obama would first cross paths a few years later.

Alas, the Ghetto Cruiser wasn't long for this world. One night in early 1984, at a party that my former girlfriend was throwing for her current boyfriend, I ran into a guy I recognized as a mechanic at the garage that shared custody rights to the Ghetto Cruiser. He half-jokingly told me that the owner was putting his kids through college on my repair bills, That money, I decided on the spot, should have been putting me through college.

I got home that night the same way I got home during most of my tenure as the Ghetto Cruiser's caretaker—by walking. Scott lived in the same general direction, so he headed out of the party with me. Chicago was stuck between winter and spring. It was raining. As we walked west on Waveland Avenue, we could hardly believe our luck: one of the gates at Wrigley Field was slightly ajar.

We slipped inside, expecting at every footstep to be encountered by a security guard, but none appeared. We followed the sound of machinery as far as we dared. Peaking around a corner, we saw a group of welders laboring beneath the stands, assembling new seating rows and disassembling old ones. We headed back into the darkness, up the ramp into the ballpark. We made our way down the aisle and slipped under the railing onto the field. We looked at each other in disbelief. We were standing on sacred ground.

The tarmac was spread over the infield and the rain was picking up intensity. Brilliant, staccato bursts escaped from the entrance tunnels adjacent to the welders' work area, bathing the field in strobe lighting. We sprinted around the covered basepaths, over and over again, in the surreal motion-picture flickering of welding light, sliding head first across home plate until the tarmac had been transformed into a pond.

When our clothes couldn't hold another drop of water, we knelt at home plate and performed an impromptu ceremony. We urged the rain gods to end the playoff drought for the Cubs, who hadn't sniffed the postseason since losing the 1945 World Series. Scott insisted that we should sacrifice something, preferably a goat, to rid the Cubs of their longstanding hex—the Curse of the Billy Goat.

I thought it unlikely that we'd find a goat on the premises and, being a Cincinnati Reds fan, I wasn't inclined to look for one. In order to expedite matters, I offered up another sacrifice: the Ghetto Cruiser.

True to my word, I called the garage the next day and told them not to bother with the current repairs. The owner said he was going to miss the old rust bucket, probably because it meant that his kids would now have to attend state colleges. So I told him to keep her. He laughed. He told me he'd have it scrapped as a favor.

And so it came to pass. The Cubs won 96 games during the 1984 regular season (25 more victories than the previous year) and were two games up on the San Diego Padres in the National League Championship

Series when the curse returned. We should have looked harder for a goat.

A couple of decades later, I was visiting my parents in Ohio when my only nephew, Ian, launched into a tantrum. My brother Patrick threatened to ground him, which only caused a bigger hissy fit. Exasperated, Patrick packed Ian into his car and drove him home for an early bedtime.

They were scarcely out of the door when my dad and I burst into laughter, reveling in the karma that had returned to bite Patrick in the ass after his demonic childhood. When we finally caught our breath, I asked Dad if my lack of procreativity had denied him the same grandfatherly come-uppance.

He thought about it for a second and, probably not wanting to say something he'd regret, went silent. Mom chimed in from the kitchen.

"You should have seen the smirk on your father's face when he signed over that Ford to you back in college."

4

The Lackademic Journey of a Sub-Genius

In the glorious days when childhood competition was viewed as character-building, our hours were filled with winner-take-all contests: jaw-rattling dodgeball games; whiffle ball games that couldn't be abandoned until ties were broken, sunlight be damned; and one game—Smear the Queer—that was more misogynous than homophobic, since girls were verboten and the guys who liked to bake ginger cookies in home ec classes weren't stupid enough to play. For that matter, it wasn't much of a game, the sole object being to gang-tackle the guy who was stupid enough to catch a ball thrown skyward by the idiot who was just gang-tackled.

In that era of mano a mano, one day loomed above all others on every second-grader's calendar: IQ Test Day.

On the day the results arrived at 531 Stanbery Avenue, my mother almost fainted. She checked and rechecked the address, the spelling of my name and my social security number. But there was no getting around it: Her oldest son had scored a few points shy of genius level.

Since all the scores were first mailed to the school, I knew what was coming and had a few days to map out a strategy. As far as I could tell, all the advantages in the grace period between the time the school received our IQ results and the moment our parents opened the mail belonged to the dumb kids.

One girl, for example, cobbled a successful strategy to be excluded from dodgeball games. Her mother, convinced that a few more rubber balls to the noggin could undermine the thin buffer zone between her daughter's IQ and those of the kids who rode the short bus, sent a note to the principal pleading for her daughter to beg out of extreme phys ed sports.

But I couldn't figure any angle in which my near-genius status was going to benefit me whatsoever.

Sure enough, Mom's joy upon reading the IQ report was quickly displaced by speculation. If she told her friends that I was a genius instead of an almost-genius, would it get back to the IQ people that she was taking liberties with their scoring system? In what area had I fallen short where real geniuses had succeeded? Was our paternal grandfather, the mysterious man who had fathered my father during a wham-bam-thank-you-ma'am marriage to our restless grandmother, a savant of some sort?

My brother Patrick piled on with a theory of his own: I was adopted. He worked the angle so hard that it became obvious to me and our sister Erin that Patrick had some deep-rooted issues around adoption. We eventually brought Patrick to tears when we doctored a comic-book birth certificate to suggest that he was forfeited by his real parents, a fictitious Jewish couple we called the Schottensteins, because of his chronic bed-wetting.

I cursed the six points separating me from a true genius, because a true genius probably would have been able to devise a plot to ease the expectation of straight As until eternity. As a sub-genius, I decided to focus my lobbying efforts on other issues that were cramping my style as a seven-year-old. I actually made a list, but I misplaced it during the final editing process. Fortunately, I was an almost-genius and had an almost-photographic memory.

First up was my 9 p.m. curfew. I approached the bench and pleaded for an extra hour, reasoning that I could fill my head with hundreds of hours of informative PBS shows each year—and possibly make up some of that ground betwixt where I stood and genius-land, should I ever run across an IQ test again.

I thought I had a shot with that one, since PBS was the only one of the four existing channels at the dawn of the '70s that our mother didn't think was immoral on some level. But my parents just laughed. With three kids and a fourth on the way, 9 p.m. was their golden hour. That motion would have failed even if Jesus Christ and Albert Einstein had been sitting had promised to tutor me between 9 and 10 p.m.

Next up: *Love, American Style* and *The Dating Game*, two wildly popular TV shows that my mother deemed pure filth and were banned in our house, at least for the kids. I opened my case by agreeing, in theory, that more impressionable minds might misinterpret some of the risqué humor that characterized the show, but ...

"Over my dead body," Mom interrupted, then sent me to bed so that she and Dad could critique *The Dating Game*.

"I'm not done yet," I said.

"Yes you are," she countered. "I found your little extortion list in the basement. So let me expedite the process for you. No, you're not going to suddenly be allowed to drink Pepsi Cola. That stuff rots your teeth. You're allowed one Fanta (the discount soda Mom bought for us) when you pack your lunch, but if you buy your lunch at school you'll drink milk."

She popped open a Pepsi as she hit her stride.

"As for next item: No gum, either. Patrick is driving us to the poor house with all his cavities. You've done one thing right in your whole life: You haven't gotten any cavities," she said, apparently forgetting the near-genius status that gotten me the audience with Her Holiness in the first place. "You know why? Because you don't drink Pepsi and you don't chew gum around the house. And don't think I don't know about all those cardboard sticks of gum you're shoving in your face when you buy your baseball cards. I'm not as dumb as I look. So consider yourself lucky that you're not being grounded for disobeying me on the gum issue."

That was that. Another whirlwind encounter with Judge Jane had ended badly for the plaintiff. I had come to the negotiating table armed to the teeth … and slunk away empty-handed and counting my blessings that I wasn't facing sanctions. Such were the rewards of near-genius.

Because St. Thomas The Apostle was a relatively isolated academic environment, I held up pretty well under the standard I had inadvertently set for myself. I kept busy with sports, playing basketball for St. Thomas and flag football for Maryland Avenue Elementary, the public school in my neighborhood.

A GOOD LOOK BEFORE DARK

When seventh grade rolled around, however, I wanted to play tackle football and convinced my parents to let me transfer to Bexley Junior High, which, being tuition-free, was an easy sell. That turned out to be a strategic mistake. It turned out my football career had peaked at age 11.

The transition from big fish in a small pond to guppy in a lake was humbling, so I tried to fit in by downplaying the brainiac thing. I got the first sub-B grade of my life—a D in science—in seventh grade. In earlier years, Mom would have sent me to my room for life.

By that point, however, she was dealing with a bigger threat to her reputation as a procreator of near-geniuses: Patrick, who was whip-smart but utterly disengaged by the academic process. In those days, we were encouraged to protect textbooks by making our own covers for them, usually from a brown-paper sack. One year, Patrick drew pictures of what appeared to be clouds on most of his do-it-yourself covers. He admitted under questioning, however, that they were actually piles of shit.

Thus did I begin practicing the most dangerous of human endeavors: cutting corners. By the time I graduated high school across town at Bishop Watterson, I ranked just 77th in a class of 231—a placement I remember only because my father had co-signed a student loan for college that gave a favorable interest rate for those who finished in the top one-third of their class. Had I slid to 78th, I wouldn't have qualified.

The spiral continued at DePaul University, where I flunked a class, for the first time in my life, in my inaugural semester. I'm not sure how I let a counselor talk me into taking German when I had taken two years of French in high school, but I'm even more befuddled as to how I let him talk me into taking it at 8 a.m. It was the last time I scheduled a class before 10 a.m., with the exception of my sophomore year, when I had to re-take the same 8 a.m. German 101 class to erase the F from my record. I got a C the second time around. *Verpiss dich*, Professor Adams!

In my sophomore year, I took a journalism class taught by a *Chicago Sun-Times* investigative reporter, Gene Mustain, who later moved to New York and wrote a couple of books about mobster John Gotti. My world was rocked. I knew, almost immediately, that I wanted to pursue the life of a newspaper reporter. Trouble was, Mustain's class was the only one the university offered.

I loved DePaul, but knew that I had to transfer. I was rejected by the University of North Carolina. Southern Illinois University was my Plan B. The whole process turned out to be a blessing in disguise, however, because SIU had a stellar journalism school. I have no idea how my parents and I would have afforded tuition at North Carolina. But since I remained in Chicago to continue working in the summers following my freshman and sophomore years, I qualified as a resident of Illinois. In-state tuition at SIU was less than $1,000 a semester.

I packed up the Ghetto Cruiser in August of 1982 and headed south on I-55 for the flat-as-a-board, 350-mile downstate trip to Carbondale, a town named for the coal that once served as its life blood.

There's a heavy Egyptian influence in southern Illinois, which is roughly defined as the area south of where I-64 dissects the state en route to St. Louis.

Abraham Lincoln referred to the area as "Egypt," which morphed into "Little Egypt" in the 20th century.

A GOOD LOOK BEFORE DARK

At the confluence of the Ohio and Mississippi Rivers in the southern tip of the state, for instance, lies the town of Cairo (Americanized to "Kay-roh" in Illinois) which was the destination of the fugitive slave, Jim, in Mark Twain's *The Adventures of Huckleberry Finn*. There's also a Thebes, Ill., as well as a Karnak, which is named for an Egyptian temple. Twenty-five miles from campus is the Lake of Egypt. SIU's sports teams are known as the Salukis: odds are that many biblical references to dogs were actually references to Salukis, the likenesses of which can be found carved into Egyptian pyramids.

My primary interest in the whole theme was the *Daily Egyptian*, SIU's student newspaper, which had a circulation of 33,000. When I transferred, I was under the assumption that the *Daily Egyptian* was part of the curriculum for every one admitted to SIU's School of Journalism.

Not so, I found out upon arrival. Each spring, highly competitive tryouts were held for staff positions for the subsequent academic year. I had missed them. This was a source of major consternation, since I was transferring as a junior and would have just two years to amass enough experience—and the right kind of newspaper clips—to get a job after graduation.

I knew exactly one person at SIU, a school I had never seen until rolling into town two days before classes started. Among a student enrollment of 23,000, I was acquainted only with Jackie Rodgers, whose compact build made her ideally suited to the game of lacrosse, at which she excelled. Jackie's angelic, freckled face was the source of unending consternation for her, since she was invariably the person in any group in which she circulated most likely to get carded, even in the bars with the laxest enforcement (18 was the entry age in Carbondale watering holes). A bouncer once told Jackie that he felt like he was earning his pay when she showed up.

Jackie transferred from DePaul a year before me, and for the same reason: to pursue a journalism degree. At DePaul, she had worked a part-time gig as a security guard at Clifton Hall, the dormitory from which I was unceremoniously evicted at the end of freshman year. Jackie and I spent countless late-night hours at the front desk talking about sports, a subject at which she was more versed than any girl I'd ever known.

Over the course of a year, those 2 a.m. lobby conversations became an invaluable source of information, since I was able to observe first-hand which girls were inclined to take guys up to their rooms. When I was unsure about the proclivities of a girl in whom I was interested, Jackie would fill me in with deep background. Every once in a while she'd dissuade me with tidbits such as "she's out of your league" or "she's only into athletes."

To my utter delight, I found Jackie's name in the masthead of the first *Daily Egyptian* printed in the 1982-83 academic year. She was listed as the sports editor. Upon reading that, I sprinted across campus to the newspaper's offices in the Mass Communications Building. I was in luck. Jackie was working and, to say the least, surprised to see me. She had no idea that I had transferred. I wasted little time in outlining my dilemma.

Jackie smiled as I wrapped up my story. "You might be in luck," she said. "One of the guys who made my staff in the spring decided not to come back to school."

It wasn't a handout, however. Jackie told me there already were two applicants for the position. If I wanted to throw my hat in the ring, Jackie said, I'd have to file my candidacy with the faculty managing editor of the *Daily Egyptian*. She pointed across the newsroom to a rail-thin, chain-smoking sexagenarian with a heavily creased forehead whose gray temples represented the last stand of a follicle-desertion movement. The smoldering coals that served as his eyes were evident from across the newsroom, even under heavy eyelids, as if the sediment of decades of cynicism was collecting there. Through the glass wall of his office, I could see him gesticulating wildly at the phone into which he was screaming.

"I'd better go tag along and introduce you," Jackie quickly decided.

She waited until the phone call was complete, then marched with me in tow and rapped on the door.

"Goddammit, what is it?" was the first thing I ever heard uttered by Bill Harmon, the man who was to transform me into a journalist by means of a method with which I had become highly acquainted as a Catholic: unadulterated fear.

Our first meeting was brief. Mr. Harmon had no use for me until I was actually a member of the newspaper's staff, so I, like the other two candidates, was assigned a story the following week—in my case, a feature on the women's softball team.

At the end of the week, Mr. Harmon judged each article and informed Jackie that mine was the least disastrous of the trio. I was offered a staff position, which, I was delighted to learn, was a paid gig at twice the prevailing minimum wage. That meant I wouldn't have to get another warehouse or proofreading job to support my bad habits. Such jobs would have been exponentially more difficult to find in remote Carbondale than in Chicago.

My grades soon became of little consequence. The

newsroom became the center of my world, even on days when I didn't have a story due. Editors at the newspapers where I would be applying after I got my degree would be judging me by my reporting skills and how I could turn a phrase. My GPA would be all but irrelevant to them. Empowered with that knowledge, I took the maximum permitted number of pass/fail classes, where a D was as good as an A. I attended other classes intermittently, as well, not all that concerned with getting Cs if I couldn't bullshit my way to a better grade.

And bullshit I did. Years later, while helping my siblings put my parents' estate in order, I found a box containing dozens of *Daily Egyptian* articles that I had authored. In the same box were two unpublished papers I'd written for a music class. One had received an A, the other a B+. They were reviews of two concerts: a Chicago-area symphony and a jazz concert in Wisconsin. Reading them 25 years later, I was dismayed that I couldn't remember a single detail from either event. Eventually, it dawned on me why; I hadn't attended either. I'd simply made up the reviews, generously sprinkling in keywords that we had learned in class.

I admit to taking similarly disingenuous routes to other As and Bs during my collegiate days. The pre-Internet era was not without its advantages. Namely, it was a lot harder for professors, associate profs and teaching assistants to verify their students' work before everything was online. My M.O. was to go to the library and check out a book or two on the subject at hand— say, the Reconstruction Era that followed the Civil War—and use those publications' bibliographies as my own, throwing in some books I completely made up. It was tough for a professor to refute a quote from a source he couldn't find. I rationalized my academic fraud on the grounds that general education classes were simply an assembly line; at the end of the day, the car need only start.

Journalism classes were another matter. I took those seriously. I was passionate about being a reporter. All the rest was merely stuff I had to get through en route to a degree.

I also had to get through Bill Harmon, the Vince Lombardi of editors. Mr. Harmon arrived at his office early every day, spreading each edition of the *Daily Egyptian* across his desk and marking up most of the articles in red before tacking the entire 32 pages or so on the wall. Everyone on the staff entered the newsroom with trepidation, praying that his/her article had been spared the blood-colored edits. An "Okay" or "Not bad" scribbled over the top of the article was high praise, cause for gloating for the rest of the day. But such plaudits were few and far between.

More common were the comments that could cut a would-be journalist like a scalpel: "Subjective statement!" … "Run-on sentence." … "Pick a tense and stick with it." … "Conjugation: It's not just for third graders." … "I'm sure Mr. Strzynski would be interested in your new spelling for his name." … "Is this an accurate quote?" … and so on.

Then there were the two words which caused our bowels to quake, always written in caps: "SEE ME."

It was best to get it over with. (Apologies to Mr. Harmon for ending that sentence in a preposition). And if it was a factual mistake, you best pray to your gods.

"Ahhhhh, Mr. Higgins." Mr. Harmon bellowed to the entire newsroom when catching sight of me after one such transgression. "The man who elevated a 'graduate assistant' to 'coach' in today's edition has graced us with his presence at last! While you're possessed of such powers, Mr. Higgins, would you mind promoting me to the goddamn board of regents? Because I could use the pay raise if I'm going to have to deal with this kind of horse shit. Why don't you step into my office and we can discuss *your* title, Mr. Higgins?"

I wisely holstered an urge to question whether regents were paid or volunteer positions.

Every once in a while someone would emerge from Mr. Harmon's office in tears. But you grew to love him as you earned his respect, incrementally and begrudgingly.

I knew that day had come at the outset of my senior year. I had taken a year off school to get my financial act together. When I returned, I faced the same dilemma I had encountered upon my transfer: tryouts for the student paper had taken place in the spring. This time, there was no vacated staff position on the student newspaper into which I could backslide.

I had no idea what to do. I couldn't show two-year-old clips to potential employers after graduation. I needed to be producing fresh articles as a senior. Panic began to set it in when Irish luck intervened once more.

The semester was several weeks old when I dropped by Mr. Harmon's office, mere minutes before the deadline he had imposed for submitting a report for his 400-level journalism class. The office was empty, so I laid the report on his desk and turned to leave. That's when I noticed the note hanging on his door. It was from his secretary. It had been folded over in an attempt at privacy, but the tape had given way, and the note was unfurled for anyone lurking around Mr. Harmon's office at 5 p.m. on a Friday to ogle.

A GOOD LOOK BEFORE DARK

Bill – Got a call from Scott Monserud, sports editor at the S.I. He's created a part-time staff position for one of our savviest undergrads … do you have any recommendations?"

The S.I. was the *Southern Illinoisan*, the daily paper which served the six dozen cities and towns in Little Egypt. I could scarcely believe my eyes. The only thing I feared more than the repercussion for confiscating Mr. Harmon's private note was somebody else seeing it. So I snatched it from his door and began a desperate, room-to-room manhunt throughout the Mass Communications Building, the reports lying on his desk evidence that he had yet to begin his weekend.

I finally tracked him down in the basement, talking to one of his colleagues outside the studio in the broadcast journalism department. It was ground upon which I rarely treaded. The talking heads had their turf. We had ours. We print journalists didn't think it was an accident that they were relegated to the basement.

"Mr. Higgins," said Mr. Harmon, who never called students by their first name. "Are you down here to relieve me of my burden by pursuing a broadcasting career?"

I laughed nervously. "No, sir," I replied. "I, um, turned in my report and, um, I …"

"Well, I can see why you're steering clear of broadcast journalism," Mr. Harmon countered. "Out with it, Mr. Higgins."

I handed him the note, profusely apologizing for having it in my possession as I was doing so.

He slid his reading glasses over his nose and looked up within seconds. I could never get over how quickly he consumed words. He could red-line an article in less time than it took me to merely read it.

I felt sick to my stomach, sure that my chosen career was about to be waylaid before it began. Seconds became hours. I could feel the nausea rising into my throat.

"I'd be happy to recommend you for the position, if that's what you're asking, Mr. Higgins," Mr. Harmon said, the happiest words I had heard in my life—until those that followed: "You have the makings of a fine journalist, Mr. Higgins."

I was stupefied.

"Th-th-thank you, Mr. Harmon," I stammered, embarrassed at the tears I was desperately fighting to hold back. "I'll try not to let you down."

As was the case two years earlier, the recommendation merely got my foot in the door. It turned out that Mr. Harmon had undertaken the same discussion with four other candidates from SIU's J-School. I didn't care. I was still glowing from his words when I got a call from the editor mentioned on the note, Scott Monserud, informing me that there would be an elimination write-off among the five candidates. As far as I knew, I was the only one who had been down this road before. I entered the fray with supreme confidence.

Once more, I lucked out. I became the first undergraduate staff member of the sports staff of the *Southern Illinoisan.*

So it was that my senior year became an unconventional one. For obvious reasons, the student paper, the *Daily Egyptian,* was only concerned with Southern Illinois University sports. The local paper, conversely, drew advertising dollars by blanketing the high school sports scene for hundreds of square miles. While my friends were spending their weekends excising brain cells on Carbondale's Strip (the section of Illinois Avenue lined with bars), I was becoming intimately familiar with the highways and back roads of Little Egypt. I spent practically every Friday night— and quite a few Saturdays during basketball season— driving to ball games in towns like Anna, Benton, Carterville, Cairo, Centralia, DuQuoin , Eldorado, Harrisburg, Marion, Metropolis, McLeansboro, Mt. Vernon, Murphysboro, Nashville, Pinckneyville, Sparta, Vienna and West Frankfort.

The Ghetto Cruiser had been replaced, against all odds, by an even more unreliable mode of transportation—an AMC Gremlin, my first stick-shift, which I bought with Pell Grant money. I became a human GPS unit when it came to navigating the southern third of Illinois, a skill that braced me for thousands more miles on the back roads of south Georgia as a sportswriter for the *Savannah Morning News & Evening Press*. Later, in service of the *Phoenix Gazette*, I memorized the web of desert roads crawling across central Arizona.

It was a transitional time at newspapers. Laptops were just appearing on the scene, but the technology for transmitting stories—through "couplers" that attached to both ends of a conventional telephone line—was still dicey. Even when we were lucky enough to check out one of the *Southern Illinoisan*'s two laptops, which were merely word processors in those pre-Internet days, they often served no greater purpose than facilitating legible notes during games.

To file our stories, we generally had to drive with considerable urgency to the newsroom in Carbondale. Over the course of my senior year, that involved speeding down hundreds of miles of pitch-black country roads. That very exercise cost one of my colleagues his life. Rushing to reach Carbondale from the south on Route 51, he was understandably discombobulated when an owl smashed into the windshield of his VW Bug. He steered into a tree and was killed instantly.

Although I was on staff at the *Southern Illinoisan* for only nine months—the duration of my senior year— my editor would be part of my life for many years to come. Nine years after he hired me in Carbondale, Scott Monserud hired me as a freelance reporter for the *Fort Worth Star-Telegram*, a gig that I was able to parlay into a staff position as an NFL beat writer. I even taught his daughter Allie how to ride a bike. It took all of one afternoon and ended years of frustration on the part of Scott and his wife to do the same.

But Allie was still a toddler in the Carbondale days. Her father had assembled a tight-knit staff in the sports department, which on weekends included several of my fellow students at SIU, stringers who covered high school games and worked the phones taking results from the games we didn't cover. Because our schedules were so out of step with everyone else's, we relied on each other for a social life on the weekends.

More often than not, that took the form of an all-night poker game. We pooled our cash and the first guy to wrap up his story went to the liquor store to purchase two 750-milliliter bottles of cheap gin, twin towers of gut-twisting intoxication, along with several bottles of tonic. We'd then meet, on a rotating basis, at somebody's abode around 2 a.m. That usually meant Scott's A-frame in Carterville or my trailer, perched on the outskirts of Carbondale above the railroad tracks on which Arlo Guthrie's famed *City of New Orleans* train rambled by several times a day. There's nothing quite as noxious as seeing the sun rise over Nowhere, Illinois with the taste of cheap gin ingrained on your tongue and exuding from all pores.

A GOOD LOOK BEFORE DARK

It was after one such session in the late spring of 1985, with my graduation rapidly approaching, that I came to clarity on two matters: I would never again drink gin; and I would, as much as possible, avoid jobs that required me to work mornings. Sunsets never fail to leave me filled with wonder and awe. Sunrises don't have much of a finish.

But the sunset of my academic career was a dud and, much like the rest of my non-journalism pursuits at SIU, filled with deceit. I left Carbondale without a degree.

It went down like this: when I returned to school after my financial hiatus in 1984, I wasn't a true senior, by Southern Illinois University's standards. If I wanted to graduate in a year, I would have to jam three semesters' worth of credit into two. There was no room for error, and my plan began to unravel when I flunked a class by showing up at the wrong time for the final exam, a result of juggling too many balls.

But I had already been approved to participate in the graduation ceremony, during which those parading to the stage in their caps and gowns received only an empty diploma case; the degree itself was mailed at a later date, after the university processed final exam grades and   more importantly to SIU's revenue stream—verified that all tuition and outstanding parking tickets had been paid. The graduation ceremony was mere pomp, ideal for my circumstances.

Nobody but my DePaul buddy, Scott Davis, was any the wiser that I was three credits shy of a degree. I had no intention of scuttling my parents' plans to see their first-born graduate (despite the fact that their second-born, Erin, had beat me to the punch by a semester when I took the year off). I easily could have remedied the mess by staying in Carbondale for the summer and taking an algebra class, something my wages at the *Southern Illinoisan* easily would have covered.

But, as the pièce de résistance in a jambalaya of stupidity, I made plans to go to Phoenix to share an apartment with another buddy from DePaul … and trade a momentous career start for a low-level construction gig. Like many of the bad decisions in my life, the karma was instant. A month later, I was balancing on a beam three stories above the ground with a tool belt around my waste, broiling in 115-degree heat and picking nail-sized splinters out of my hands and knees, begging for a quick death.

I had crashed and burned within sight of the finish line, my punishment, I figured, for all the bullshit I had submitted as course work en route to my destination.

As I suspected, nobody in the journalism world bothered to check the assertion on my résumé that I had graduated. Four years after my fake matriculation, while working as a reporter in Savannah, I put the matter to rest by taking an algebra course at Armstrong State College. Because the school operated on a trimester system while Southern Illinois was semester-based, the three credits for the class didn't quite transfer evenly. The counselor at SIU advised me to sign up for an additional one-credit class at Armstrong State—any class at all would do—and my problem would be solved.

Things happen for a reason, and my years of angst led me to what may have been the coolest class offered by any school in the country: a one-credit course called "Survival 101." It was taught by an Army Ranger sergeant from Hunter Army Air Base, just down the road from Armstrong State.

When we weren't rappelling down the front of

Armstrong State's wooden tower, we spent much of our class time traipsing the woods behind the college. There, we learned to make drinking water where none was apparent, to differentiate an edible plant from a poisonous one, and the art of shelter-building. Thus were the seeds of my love of hiking planted, though it would be another decade before they took root.

I took the final exam for my algebra course on a Friday. The professor was acquainted with my unique situation and told me to hang around a few minutes while she graded the test. She informed me that my final grade would be an A.

The finish line beckoned once again.

The final exam for Survival 101 was the dream of every guy who had played with GI Joes or blown up plastic green soldiers with fire crackers as a boy: We would be transported by Blackhawk helicopter from the Armstrong State campus to nearby Fort Stewart, which, unlike the urban Hunter Army Air Base, was rife with wooded areas. There we were to be paired into two-person teams and spend a weekend testing our newfound survival skills (in an easily monitored area).

But as we were gathering in the parking lot on that Saturday morning, the good sergeant and his colleagues were being deployed to Panama to capture its dictator, Manuel Noriega, a former CIA operative who had gone rogue. Our helicopter was routed elsewhere. Nobody bothered to tell the dozen or so members of the Armstrong State College Survival 101 class. An hour rolled by, then another. With our final grades on the line, we were reticent to leave.

Finally, a black SUV bearing an Army insignia rolled into the parking lot. It pulled to a stop in front of our group. A young officer emerged.

"Since you're the only ones in the parking lot, I'm assuming you're the class awaiting transport to Fort Stewart," he said. We confirmed.

He then told us that a "military situation" had forced the cancellation of our final exam weekend. "But," he added, "the sergeant wanted me to tell you that he was honored to train with all of you—and that each of you would be receiving an A for the course."

He got back in his vehicle and disappeared.

Thus did my academic career, with its pathetic downward spiral, end in a parking lot. I had built a web of deceit around my fake graduation years earlier, so there was nobody with whom to share the moment when the real deal was accomplished. I thought back to St. Thomas, and what the 7-year-old, almost-genius version of me would have thought about the guy standing in the parking lot at Armstrong State 20 years later. "Disappointed" came to mind.

My degree, at long last, came in the mail. I had been under the assumption since transferring to Southern Illinois that I was pursuing a Bachelor of Arts, like the preponderance of journalism degrees in the U.S. The universe had a more fitting award in mind. It turned out that SIU was one of the few schools to offer a Bachelor of Science in the field. Thus was my degree designation an apropos "B.S."

5

Freeflailing

We were 10,000 feet above Xenia, Ohio, and the winds weren't quite right.

"Take it up a little higher," Mike screamed at the pilot above the noise of the turbo-propped aircraft.

"Relax" he said to me, sensing my edginess. "It'll be a few more minutes."

"What's your mantra?" Dan said to me, trying to keep me focused on the task at hand.

"TV guys are pussies!" I screamed.

"Excellent!" he replied back, patting my shoulders in approval.

Two weeks earlier, the sportscaster on Columbus, Ohio's highest-rated newscast had been exactly where I was now—crouched in a Cessna 182, awaiting his cue to jump—when he exercised his right to bail out. Worse still, his cameraman was with him, and the story they had wasted a day pursuing was scrapped. Like me, the sportscaster and his cameraman were skydiving virgins, so like me had spent hours training inside a classroom and then practicing their moves on a field beside the runway. They had wasted all of it. I was determined not to be a TV pussy when the zero hour came.

Unlike the TV dudes, however, none of my editors would have been the wiser if I changed my mind. Working at a chain of suburban newspapers in my hometown a year after my fake graduation, I had been assigned to write a story about the Fusion Skydiving Team, which had nearly pulled off a Cinderella story by giving the vaunted Golden Knights, the Army's perennial powerhouse team, a scare at the U.S. Nationals four-person competition in 1986.

My idea was to cover the story from the point of view of a student learning the craft from Dan Brodsky-Chenfield, a guy my age who was one of the stars of the Fusion team that trained out of bucolic Xenia, so I planned to jump with Dan. My editor liked the idea, but the chain's lawyers shot down the idea based on concerns that I might try to go rogue and end up as fertilizer on the cornfields of Xenia. I was free to write a story, but I'd have to do so with my feet firmly planted on terra firma.

But when I got there and Dan told me the story about my reluctant TV colleague, I took it upon myself to defend the honor of the media. Having made the decision to go rogue (thus proving the lawyers correct), I figured it couldn't hurt if I piled on another fire-able offense by forgoing the tandem jump preferred by first-time skydivers, wherein the novice is closely attached by harness to an experienced jumper. I wanted to jump solo, or freefall, like the big boys.

Thus, just a year out of college with an almost-degree, was I about to commit my first act of professional fraud. From cases we'd studied at Southern Illinois, fraud traditionally involved not showing up and writing as if you did, or fabricating quotes, or similarly shameless brands of laziness or indifference. In my case, however, I needed to figure out a way to write around the six hours I would spend in jump school and then hurtling myself out of the single-engine plane—as if none of it had happened.

But just as I was about to jump out of the plane that I wasn't officially riding in, Mike Hossey, my co-trainer, came back from the cabin to inform me that the winds at our planned jumping altitude of 10,000 feet were too dicey; we would climb to 14,000 feet and reassess the conditions up there. Having summoned all my reserves of courage and adrenaline in order to appear as a more fearless brand of journalist than my TV counterpart, I was forced to ease up on my internal throttle ... and then summon my manhood all over again when we reached our recalibrated altitude.

Since I was the lone student in that day's ground school, we didn't waste the fuel on the Beechcraft 18 cargo plane that would have transported a bigger class to their destination aloft. Instead, we were airborne in the smaller Cessna 182, which meant my exit was a little more complicated.

I'd have to slide along two strut bars positioned three feet apart—one for my hands, one for my feet—attached to the wing. That seemed ludicrous enough, but then we came to the part of the class where I was informed how I was supposed to set the jump itself in motion: when I was ready to detach myself from the strut bars framing the wing, I was to turn to my right and make eye contact with Mike, who was to precede me onto the strut in the role of secondary jumpmaster. I was then to turn to the left and gaze into the steely eyes of Dan, my primary jumpmaster, then perform three deep knee bends and hurl myself backwards into the abyss.

"Very funny," I said in the classroom when this scheme was laid out. "You had me until the knee bends. Now you're just messing with the new guy, right?"

I was assured that, given the roaring cacophony of wind and engine turbulence, the three-count of calisthenics was the most efficient form of communication.

"Then I just launch?" I asked.

"Yes," Mike said. "Just three. Please. For the love of god."

Mike, I came to find out, was still a bit jumpy from an experience a year or so earlier, when, against his better judgment, he had agreed to allow a middle-aged woman who was freshly liberated from an overbearing husband to sign up for a freefall rather than a tandem jump on her inaugural skydive. It turned into a ballet class, with her counting off 53 knee bends before summoning the courage to let go. Because she had paid extra to have the whole thing filmed—presumably as some sort of "F.U." to her ex—the exact number of false starts wasn't a matter of conjecture. Mike counted them off in the film room.

I feared a similar display of cowardice more than I feared the unknown of plunging earthbound at 32-feet-per-second-squared. I knew I wouldn't be able to live with myself if, like the TV guy, I made the plane turn around at the moment of truth. So I did what was to become habitual for me in moments of truth: I overcompensated.

As we rehearsed, I disconnected from the plane as

A GOOD LOOK BEFORE DARK

I came out of my third knee bend. Mike later said that he'd never seen anybody separate himself from the plane with so much conviction. Dan said it looked like I'd been shot from a cannon. They weren't being complimentary. As I would later find out, it's much better for a novice to begin a backwards freefall by simply letting go and letting gravity take over (which is why they call it a freefall). I, on the other hand, apparently began my routine with something Greg Louganis might have attempted to impress Olympic judges. And that's pretty much where it all started going south.

Terminal velocity, the speed at which gravity and wind resistance are equal, is about 120 m.p.h. for humans. That is, humans who are aerodynamically splayed correctly for a freefall, which was about 90 percent of the reason for all the pre-jump training we did that day. It's really a pretty simple position, one that's on display in yoga classes every day, whereby the arms and legs are spread and positioned above one's abdominal core, much like a professional wrestler would look as he leaps off the ropes to finish off his prone opponent.

It's possible for competitive skydivers, like Mike and Dan, to reach terminal velocities of 200 m.p.h. or greater by turning themselves into human bullets— swooping, they call it. Contrary to the impression given by Keanu Reeves's character in one of the all-time adrenaline-junkie movies, *Point Break*, this generally takes months, and sometimes years, to perfect.

As Mike and Dan discovered that day, however, there's a more expeditious route to the 200 m.p.h. barrier: by becoming a human anvil.

Had I opted for filming that day, I certainly could have turned it into viral gold three decades on. Viewers would have seen me plunging, ass over teakettle, for the better part of two miles, with little more control than a 200-pound boulder would have displayed. They also would have seen Mike and Dan exhausting their full repertoire of tricks as they approached and withdrew, swooping over and over in repeated attempts to correct the posture of their whirling dervish of a student (and avoid being knocked unconscious).

My accelerated velocity, the guys estimated, probably trimmed 30 seconds off of what should have been a two-minute freefall. But seeing as how I was largely missing the view anyway—the small, neat rectangles of farmland below me turning into bigger and slightly less neat rectangles—it was all the same to me.

I may have been the only one of the three of us plunging toward the surface of the planet that day to think so, but I'm certain that I got the hang of it at the precise instant that I ran out of time. I vividly recall rotating into the proper inverted parabolic position, belly first, and being endlessly pleased with myself. But as in the rest of life, being endlessly pleased with oneself is usually the cue for a paradigm shift. At the moment I had corrected course, I checked the altimeter and noted that I had plummeted below 5,000 feet, the point at which I was supposed to pull the ripcord. I casually reached down to my belt to do just that. I was more than a little surprised that my parachute deployed before I had scarcely bent my elbow.

It took me a few moments to realize what had happened; Dan had gone into a swoop and pulled my ripcord for me.

As I went reeling once more, my arm became entangled in the deploying chute. Had that imaginary camera still been rolling, those YouTube viewers a generation down the pike would have seen me hanging under the canopy, my right arm held upright by a hundred silken threads. I looked like an idiot raising my hand to go the bathroom a half-mile above the ground.

Ever so carefully, cord by cord, I freed myself from the entanglement. At long last, I could enjoy the indescribable feeling of floating above the home planet. After he deployed my chute, Dan, being a hotshot, continued to freefall. He even deployed his own chute and was on the ground manning the radio transmitter before I located him. Through the receiver in my helmet, he expertly guided my use of the toggles. After all the mayhem, I dropped as softly as a dandelion seed into the middle of the landing circle.

"Looked really good there, right at the very end," Dan said while futilely attempting to suppress a laughing seizure.

"Well, I learned from the best," I said.

"Yeah, about that," Dan said. "How about free lessons for a month to *not* write a word about what happened today?"

Dan laughed again when I came clean about the directives from the lawyers that I was not to jump under any circumstances. He was decidedly relieved that I would be writing the story in a decidedly non-participatory manner.

Six years later, while training his own team for the U.S. Nationals over the Southern California desert, the plane carrying Dan Brodsky-Chenfield and his teammates crashed, killing 16 of the 22 on board. Dan awoke from a coma six weeks later and 40 pounds lighter. He went on to write an autobiography, *Above All Else*, and continued his career as a world-class skydiving coach in California—my ultimate destination.

6

Worthless Yankee Currency

My next stop was Savannah, a job which I accepted on my 25th birthday.

I arrived towing a small U-haul trailer containing my scant possessions. When I stopped by the apartment complex office to pay my rent and pick up my keys, I was thrilled to find a strapping, cornpone-fed Georgia boy in the office dropping off his monthly check as well. I introduced myself, informed him that I was new in town and asked if I could give him $20 to help me muscle my couch into my second-floor apartment. He accepted my offer graciously. Since the couch would be the last thing off the trailer and the only piece of furniture I figured I couldn't haul up the stairs myself, I asked him to meet me in an hour.

But he showed up at my doorstep within 10 minutes and helped me unpack the entire load. Twenty minutes after we started, the couch was in my apartment and the job was complete. I pulled out the $20 and added a second $20, a lot of money for me in

1987. But I considered it a bargain, and slapped the bills into his hand as I thanked him profusely for his kindness.

He looked at the money as if I'd spit in his hand. "No sir," he said, tucking them into my shirt pocket. "That's not the way it's done down here."

"Well, neighbor," I said, opening his man-paw and re-submitting my payment, "that is the way it's done where I'm from, so please accept it as a sign of my gratitude."

He screwed up his face as if he was trying to figure out a way to explain something to a 6-year-old. I recognize the flush in his cheeks as brewing anger.

"Mr. Brian," he said, despite being about my age, "the last thing you want to do on your first day in Savannah is start throwing insults around. So I'm gonna assume that isn't your intention and politely decline one last time."

I gulped, apologized and meekly returned the money to my back pocket.

"Now you wash up, and be at my place by six," he said, scribbling down an address on the other side of the complex. "My wife don't tolerate stragglers. Six o'clock sharp."

I arrived on the dot. An uncracked bottle of a bourbon I had professed to love just an hour earlier was sitting in the center of the table, surrounding by a feast of fried chicken, home-made biscuits, greens and the most mouth-watering corn-on-the-cob I had ever tasted.

My mind flashed back to a near-miss on Interstate 95 earlier that day, when I had slammed on the brakes to avoid a semi truck that swerved into the right lane with no apparent regard for the fact that I was already occupying it. Had it actually hit me? Maybe I'm dead, I thought, and this is the hereafter. Overtly friendly neighbors, great booze and amazing comfort food for eternity.

I was falling for Savannah's siren call, and it had only taken a few hours.

As if the whole thing was an apparition, I never saw my gentle giant of a neighbor, nor his wife, again. But I never forgot his kindness, nor his introduction to the genteel city of Savannah, which was as fascinating to me anthropologically and sociologically as it was impervious to the rest of the world. Over the next few years, I'd come to learn that it was appropriate, upon greeting friends and strangers, to ask not how they were, but what they were drinking.

I had agreed to plantation wages: $300 a week. With rent, food, car payments and insurance pretty well draining my meager salary, I was soon plotting a strategy to cover the cost of another major budgetary item: alcohol.

My plan was to get a job bartending. I had considerable experience and Savannah, a tourist town, was infested with bars. I was doing my due diligence, looking for the right fit by imbibing at as many watering holes as possible in my new town, when I stumbled upon an easier solution to my budgetary crisis: not paying for my drinks at all. Lacking cleavage, I pulled off that parlor trick by the only means at my disposal. I became almost-famous.

About three months into my tenure, I broke a story about a state powerhouse football team using an illegal transmitter to broadcast messages from the sideline directly into the quarterback's helmet. My story resulted in the best football team in the history of

Evans High School in Augusta forfeiting a state quarterfinal game that it had already won, cost a longtime coach his career and kept me rolling in cross-state death threats for a few weeks. Closer to home, however, I was a hero, for it was a team in the next county—the Effingham County Rebels, the losers of said quarterfinal game—that got a do-over pass into the state semifinals and took advantage by marching to the state championship game, where the Rebs finally lost (again).

In 1987, there was no such thing as "going viral." A story in a market like Savannah had to work its way through the system, from local news to state news to regional news to national news, etc. So I was as surprised as anyone when my story about a high school football game in Springfield, Georgia—along with a series of follow-up articles that showed Evans High had cheated its way to many other victories—grabbed headlines from coast to coast.

During the weeks while the story raged, I was on round-the-clock deadline to file fresh stories and update old ones. I slept mere hours in weeks. Moonlighting as a bartender was no longer an option. Nor was it a necessity. For a hot minute, as they'd say in Georgia, I was a household name everywhere in the state. As on the day I arrived in Savannah, my money was no good. Everyone who didn't want to kill me wanted to buy me drinks. That prompted the owner of one of Savannah's most popular bars to give me a nickname that far outlasted my 15 minutes of fame: "Hottest Girl in the Bar," for my ability to elicit free booze.

Criss-crossing the state while filing stories morning and night for the sports section and the front page, I fell into the detached, glassy-eyed state of insomnia. At times, five or six minutes would pass while I stared at a blank screen, fingers hovering to deliver the nothingness from my brain. I sat in editorial budget meetings without absorbing any words. I became a journalistic zombie, riding infusions of adrenaline to power past deadlines.

The dream-like sequence reached its zenith one night at a pep rally for Effingham County's appearance in the state championship game, where I was asked to make a few remarks. It didn't exactly smack of objectivity to me, but as a medium-sized paper attempting to put a lot of local papers out of business, *The Savannah Morning News & Evening Press* wasted no opportunity to fly its own banner. I had prepped for a 30-second speech. I received a 2-minute standing ovation, a sleepy-eyed Yankee engulfed in a sea of Confederate Flags, a roar so loud that the public address system was useless. What a rush. If standing ovations ever are bottled, cocaine's days are numbered. I don't know what I said, but I do remember giving up on "Savannah Morning News & Evening Press" halfway through that bulky moniker. After speaking for less than a minute, it took me 45 minutes to glad-hand and high-five my way through the masses gathered for the rather impromptu event. It was as if Johnny Walker had come marching home again.

Adrenaline is a short-lived high, and the buzz had receded before I found my car. I undoubtedly was fading fast on the 25-mile ride back to Savannah. Before progressing a mile, I found myself in the glaring lights of a county sheriff on Route 21. That's where I was forced to perform a DUI drill on the side of the road while half of Effingham County rolled by, many of them shouting expletives at the cop who had dared to pull me over. I was merely exhausted, not intoxicated, so after 10 humiliating minutes he sent me on my way.

A GOOD LOOK BEFORE DARK

The next morning, I received phone calls from a county supervisor, a mayor and some school administrators asking if I wanted to have the trooper reprimanded. I thought about it for a few seconds but decided to pass, feeling magnanimous in my mercy, like Claudius sparing the life of a fallen gladiator. This story had scaled the heights of Mount Absurdity.

Alas, I snapped.

During that long December, I was casually dating a girl who was named for a bit player in Greek mythology. Medea was a lanky brunette with curly locks down to the middle of her back and a swimmer's body bequeathed by genetics rather than exercise, which she hated. She was dying to get away from Savannah, if only for a few days. Against my better judgment, I asked if she wanted to accompany me an all-expenses paid trip to Thomaston, 200 miles away in the middle of nowhere, where I was headed for the Georgia High School Association board hearing that would decide the forfeiture matter. Just what every girl wants in a romantic getaway. I told I'd her likely be working every minute, but she took me up on the offer just the same.

I scarcely had time to talk with her. At one point, I fished a balled-up $20 bill out of my pocket and handed it to her, imploring her to enjoy all that Thomaston had to offer while I was filing a story. When I came back to our room, she was asleep in a hot bath. There was a T-shirt on the bed in my size that read, simply, "Yankee Doodle." Underneath was sketched some sort of doodle that I couldn't readily identify. Oh well. It was a nice gesture, I figured.

After two days of story-filing madness, Medea insisted on driving home after I nodded off at the wheel before we even got to the highway. I didn't wake up until we were halfway between Macon and

Savannah, then spent the rest of the trip on my Radio Shack laptop, silently typing an update.

When we arrived back in Savannah, Medea accompanied me to my apartment, where we instantly collapsed with exhaustion. She was gone when I woke up with drool on the front of my Yankee Doodle T-shirt. Yes, I was quite a catch.

She returned, dolled up and dressed to the nines, to find me eating a Spam sandwich on moldy bread. Grocery shopping had become a casualty during my 15 minutes of fame.

She greeted me with "Are you even going to take a shower?" and followed it up with "You are not wearing that disgusting thing, are you?" as she pointed to my slobber-covered Yankee Doodle T-shirt, which was now stained with mustard. That ignited a discussion in which I claimed to be baffled by anyone who would eat Spam sans mustard, while Medea claimed to be equally perplexed by anyone who would eat Spam, period.

She reminded me that we had a date to attend a party at the home of one of our copy editors, Fred, a 40-ish bachelor with bottle-thick glasses, mutton chops and the bushy moustache (but not the body) of a '70s porn star. In the newsroom, Fred was forever using double entendres that he invented, but that were unmistakably sexual in nature. "I'd like to split her headlines," he'd say after one of the females working in the paste-up room inquired about separating an overflow headline into two lines.

"Baby, pleeeeeassse," I whined to Medea. "I asked you to that party three weeks ago, before any of this craziness went down. I'm sooooooo far behind on sleep. Can we pleeeeassssse just stay home tonight and watch *MacGyver*?"

"I didn't spend two hours getting ready so we could watch *MacGyver*!" she shrieked. "I want to go out tonight! That trip to Thomaston sucked! And I don't think you really want me sitting around all night measuring you against a man like *MacGyver*. You fell asleep during foreplay yesterday!"

I was headed for the shower before she fired that last volley, the verity of which I will dispute to the grave. I fell asleep during the kissing phase, thus was not an official participant in foreplay.

While disrobing, I noticed for the first time that the "doodle" at the bottom of my shirt was, in fact, a tiny penis. Until that moment, I was under the impression that it was a badly drawn pig or rat and that the T-shirt as a whole was a thinly veiled insult to the drawing abilities of Northerners, which in my opinion was a lot stupider than it was humorous. Now I got it.

"Hey, that's pretty funny," I shouted from the bathroom, realizing as I did so that I hadn't provided any context.

"Oh yeah," she shouted back, picking up on the argument where she left off, "hearing you snoring while I was trying to make love to you was hilarious. You're such an ass!'

I spent a hot minute, in local parlance, staring into the mirror. Eight years earlier, I graduated high school with 180 athletic pounds strung across my 6-foot-2 frame. Five years after that, thanks to a diet consisting largely of Taco Bell burritos, daily-deadline stress and the heroic consumption of alcohol after meeting said deadlines, I left Carbondale at a puffy 225.

My parents' home movies of my fake graduation served as an eye-opener, and I spent the next year in gym-rat mode, peeling off those extra 45 pounds in a mere five months with twice-daily workouts and a diet consisting almost solely of canned tuna fish. I was in superb shape when I arrived in Savannah.

But just five months later, I had returned to ways of old to deal with the stress of a high school football game gone wild, and it was beginning to show. I sighed and climbed into the shower.

As I dried off, I decided that I would adopt an air of gratitude that evening, starting with my gratitude for decoding the T-shirt that Medea had given me. Had I worn it to the party, I wouldn't have heard the end of the small-dick entendres from Fred for a year. I toweled off, slipped on a pair of jeans and another of my favorite T-shirts, given to me a few months earlier by the baseball coach at Savannah's Johnson High after I suggested that Johnson might have the coolest mascot of any high school in the United States.

"That's what you're wearing?" I heard Medea say for the second time in 20 minutes. "A Johnson Atom Smashers T-shirt?"

We arrived just as Fred was regaling a group of copy editors with another of his nonsensical, leering comments. "So I said, 'yeah, go ahead and roll the presses, baby. We'll roll 'em all night long.' "

Medea recognized one of her college classmates, so I left her to fend for herself with the village idiots. At the self-serve bar, I ran into my closest friend on the newspaper staff, Don Heath, whom I hadn't seen since the craziness began. After 20 minutes of getting caught up, during which Don had to slow me down two or three times because I was talking too fast to be understood (something I heard a lot in the South), I realized that I was holding Medea's undelivered drink.

"Oh shit," I said to Don. "I'm already on double-secret probation with this girl. Walk with me out to the porch and cover for me."

Medea, however, had relocated from where I had last seen her. I was about to head back into the house when Don said "uh-oh" and pointed toward the shadows in the corner of the porch. There, seated next to Medea on a love seat and stroking her neck, was Fred.

Under normal circumstances, I like to think that maturity would have gained the upper hand, and I would have seen the situation for what it was—Medea, starved for attention, being frozen like a deer in the headlights when Fred reached his tipping point and reverted to the caveman software that was always idling just below his surface. I like to think that I strolled over, grabbed Medea's hand and removed her from harm's way, warning Fred to set his sights on lower-hanging fruit, and that we partied happily ever after.

In the real world, the events of the previous weeks had conspired to mutate my personality, which was now a boiling kettle of arrogance, omnipotence, sleep deprivation and relationship frustration.

So what actually happened was that I dumped my drink on Fred's head. And when he stood up to defend his sleazy honor, I grabbed him by his clownish suspenders, spun him around and tossed him, like a syphilitic discus, off his own porch. He hit the dirt and his head snapped backwards, striking the ground with resounding force.

The party buzz went silent. Don jumped off the porch and rushed to Fred's side.

"What the hell is wrong with you?" Don bellowed, the first time I had ever heard him raise his voice. "You could have killed him! You've lost it, Brian. Fucking lost it. You need to leave. Now."

My mother always said that God protects fools and drunks, so Fred was doubly insured that night. He rose, brushed himself off, and told me to get off his property.

I never saw Medea again. And I really didn't care.

7

Now Coming to the Plate: Vengeance

I should have struck while the iron was hot and blanketed the South with my updated résumé. Although the Evans-Effingham County drama played out in December, it was nonetheless named the runner-up for story of the year in 1987 by the *Atlanta Journal-Constitution.*

That shocked many of my colleagues around the state, who were hard-pressed to remember when the AJC had given such weight to a story that wasn't theirs (AJC sports reporter Chris Mortensen—who became better known over the ensuing decades as ESPN's NFL analyst—topped me in the AJC rankings with an investigative series about a pair of corrupt NFL agents, later turning it into a book).

The *Georgia Sportswriters Association* and *Associate Press* awarded me with story of the year designations. But my cheapskate newspaper refused to fund my trip to Atlanta for the dinner at which all the awards would be tendered, thus planting the seeds of my discontent.

The paper's idea of a merit raise was a $10-a-week bump.

Savannah is a seductress and I fell hard for her. After all, I had only been in town for four months when the story broke. By the time ambition got the better of me, opportunity had receded like the tide.

Not that being marooned in Savannah was the worst of fates. During normal times, I had a weekend day off as well as every Wednesday, when I liked to drive through the fog-shrouded marshes of Wilmington Island en route to Tybee Island, where the Savannah River empties into the Atlantic Ocean. The fog connected me to my past and, little did I know, my future.

Tybee's tides are semi-diurnal, so I got into the habit of checking the tide tables in the paper on Tuesday night and timing my excursions to correspond with the window between ebb and high tide in the afternoon. I'd plant my lawn chair at the high tide mark, with my cooler on one side and a radio tuned to WIXV (I-95) on the other. As often as not, I had the beach to myself, so I'd drink Jack Sandwiches (Jack Daniels+Coke+Jack Daniels) and sing along with .38 Special and Don Henley while my fair Irish skin turned crimson over the course of the afternoon. When the tide reached my chair, that was my cue to take one final dip and head home.

One Wednesday as high tide approached, I was cooling off with a final round of body surfing when I noticed an older couple hanging around my beach chair. There was nary another soul on the entire beach, and while they didn't look like miscreants, the fact that they were lurking around my stuff was odd.

As I approached, it became obvious they were reading something in the paper I usually brought along

A GOOD LOOK BEFORE DARK

for perusal. It turned out to be a blurb that I had read just a few minutes earlier, an update on the coach I implicated in my stories. He had been suspended with pay when I broke the story, and, according to our sister paper in Augusta on that particular Wednesday, was now resigning as football coach and athletic director.

The woman jumped as I approached from behind.

"Oh my," she said, "you scared me half to death."

They seemed genuinely embarrassed to be caught snooping around, but I was flush with Jack Sandwiches, sunshine and seawater, so I told them not to sweat it and offered them a drink. They seemed delighted by the offer. I always had extra cups in the cooler, lest I be caught unprepared when a thirsty, bikini-clad maiden or two happened upon my beach encampment, something that occurred exactly zero times during my two years of weekly sojourns to the shore.

I offered the lady my chair and the gentleman a seat on my cooler. I pulled up a spot in the sand and listened as they explained that the headline had captured their attention as they strolled by because their grandson was an athlete at Evans High School. Without tipping my hand, I told them that I was familiar with the story, since it had gotten quite a bit of play in these parts.

Over the next 90 minutes or so, as the sun dipped into the ocean and the beach faded to gray, I listened as the couple described how the forfeited football game had devastated their community. They talked of the polarizing effects of the drama, with families and friends choosing sides and assessing blame. The woman's eyes reddened as she told me of a recent falling out with her own son, the father of the Evans athlete, whom she had taken to task for defending the coaching staff. Even the members of the Columbia

County school board, her husband added, were at each others' throats.

At ground zero, Evans High School, her grandson had told them, there was more crying than if one of the students had died. It was there, in the gloaming of Tybee Island, that I truly learned of what I had wrought.

By and by, they asked me if I knew anything about the Savannah reporter that had broken the story. "I hear he's a womanizing lounge lizard," I replied. "What have you heard up there in Augusta?"

"We heard that there were death threats against him," she said.

I had forgotten that part. Oddly, I felt as if I'd just received the highest praise available to a journalist. The next day at the newspaper, I relayed my beach conversation at our weekly staff meeting, which devolved into a game of "How's Brian going to be taken out?" Don was the unofficial winner, suggesting that my corpse would receive a Jimmy Hoffa-like sendoff and be buried in the end zone of Evans High's football stadium.

None of us guessed that I'd be beaten to death by two dozen bat-wielding athletes. But that's nearly the way it went down.

In June of '88, six months after the fateful football game, the Evans High baseball team was steamrolling its way to the state baseball title, blessed by the talents of the same athletes who likely would have been football champions, as well, had I not conducted a few extra interviews on that oddest of December nights.

The best baseball team in my coverage area that season hailed from Statesboro High. As fate would have it, Evans and Statesboro crossed paths in the state quarterfinals. As I scanned the Knights' lineup a few days before the 60-mile trip to Statesboro for the deciding games in the best-of-three series, my throat tightened: the majority of the players on the roster had also had key roles on the football team. And the Evans baseball coach, whose son played both sports, was an assistant on the football team. I was headed into the eye of the storm.

After a routine Evans' victory in the baseball game (this one controversy-free) I gathered with a reporter from the Statesboro newspaper and a few TV guys from Savannah to interview the winning coach. He was halfway through his first reply to a question from one of the TV reporters when he apparently remembered something important and halted in mid-sentence.

"I done forgot to ask: Is one of you boys Brian Higgins from the *Savannah Morning News?*"

"Here we go," I thought as I raised my hand.

"Well then, son," he said, "you can just step right out of this here interview, 'cause I ain't saying a damn word to you or your newspaper."

Which is exactly what I should have done. But he called me "son," a habit of southern men that I found condescending. And now my Irish was up.

"I have the same right as any other reporter to be here," I retorted.

What followed was far from my proudest professional moment. The conversation quickly grew heated and personal ... and then escalated to the doorstep of confrontation. The coach was intent on pointing out the injustice of a carpetbagger derailing his boys from manifest destiny. I was determined to drive home the point that I was merely a credentialed witness to a brazen scheme by full-grown men, one of whom was him, to cheat the system.

With his face now a shade of red that I have since encountered only in desert sunsets, the coach mounted his final counter-attack: "You broke my kid's heart!" he screamed, spittle flying willy-nilly.

By this point, his broken-hearted son had disembarked from the nearby team bus to defend his father's honor—along with every last member of the Evans baseball team. Nearly all of them were carrying bats. It's unlikely that many of them knew who I was as they spilled from the bus, other than a reporter squaring off with their coach. But as they picked up pieces of the conversation, they all started putting a face to the byline. And it's probably safe to say they were, to a player, a few exits north of pissed.

A hundred yards away, the members of the defeated Statesboro team were plodding toward their dressing room inside the high school when they took note of their opponents exiting their bus en masse. With their own equipment in hand, the Blue Devils tore off in a pack and raced to the rescue, encircling the Evans contingent that was encircling me and the coach. Leading the Statesboro charge was Joey Hamilton, who went on to pitch 10 years in the major leagues, most notably in the San Diego Padres' rotation.

The game that just ended had been unusually chippy for a baseball contest, with neither team hiding its disdain for the other. On top of that, the Statesboro players were, unlike their opponents from Evans, largely fond of me. I was, after all, the reporter from the big city (by Statesboro standards, anyway) who had been giving them ink all season. They probably considered me to be the guy who was printing their passes to Get Laid Land.

Thus did the coach and I find ourselves at the epicenter of a potential teenage riot. In the future, I thought, it might be good policy to assign one of my stringers to cover games in which Evans High was involved. Once again, I found myself at ground zero of a maelstrom of humanity. Once again, it was all because of a game played by teens.

Just as the kettle was about to boil over, Statesboro coach Kenny Tucker pushed his way through the crowd and wedged himself between me and his spittle-spewing counterpart. Kenny was one of the most respected baseball coaches in that part of the state. He also was an assistant football coach at Statesboro, one of Effingham County's rivals, so he was intimately familiar with the backstory.

As a pre-teen paper boy with a route in a shitty neighborhood where the residents let their abused pets run wild, I had learned the hard way not to divert my gaze when a dog was in attack mode. Despite the overwhelming feeling that I was being engulfed in madness, I hadn't taken my eyes off the Evans baseball coach since his tantrum began. He seemed quite capable of inflicting corporal harm, and I was determined to give it as good as I got it.

"Brian, look at me!" Kenny barked. "Look at me!" He repeated until I unlocked my gaze on his counterpart.

"This is going to go down bad for everybody," Kenny said, looking me in the eye. "You need to be the bigger man and walk away from this."

With that, he began pushing me backwards, firmly. Whenever we met a pocket of resistance from the Evans players, the Statesboro players interceded to form a part in the crowd. After we had surged through the horde, Kenny spun me around, grabbed hold of my arm and walked me back to his office in the school. He instructed one of his assistants to herd his team into the locker room and another to stand sentry until the Evans Knights re-boarded their bus and drove away.

As my adrenaline plummeted from high tide, I was confronted by the absurdity of what had just happened. "You're a good man, Kenny," I said. "I'm really sorry I put you and your guys in that situation."

"It wasn't all you," Kenny replied. "That situation has been brewing for six months."

Seventeen years later, on the next occasion when Effingham County met Evans on the football field, a reporter from the *Augusta Herald* tracked me down in California and called to get my spin on the events of 1987, roughly the year of birth for the seniors on both teams. I was more than a little surprised to hear that there was quite a bit of residual rancor in Augusta about the way history unfolded for the Evans High football team. In truth, I didn't believe him; I figured it was the case of a young reporter trumping up some drama for his own story.

But maybe not. In 2013, more than a quarter century after the controversy, another controversy in the Georgia High School Association ranks prompted the *Atlanta Journal-Constitution* to run a story listing 10 notable forfeits of high school football games in the state over the years. The story dubbed the 1987 Evans-Effingham County debacle "the most famous forfeiture in GHSA history."

In 2002, as a reporter for the *Oakland Tribune*, I was interviewing a retired Oakland Raiders player when the unlikely topic surfaced. Ray Guy, who in 2014 would become the first punter enshrined in the Pro Football Hall of Fame, attended Thomson High School, on the outskirts of Augusta. He had already

A GOOD LOOK BEFORE DARK

retired from the NFL when the Great Evans Controversy of 1987 surfaced, but he knew all about it. When I disclosed my involvement, he asked me if I had ever set foot in Augusta. When I told him that I had not, he volunteered some advice: "If you ever do go," he said, "you might want to sneak in at night and keep your windows rolled up."

8

Why Bars Close at 2 A.M.

Like the ocean 17 miles away, McDonough's Pub was ruled by diurnal tides: the graveyard shift workers and derelicts that drank boilermakers during daylight hours; and the ink-stained employees of the *Savannah Morning News & Evening Press* who repopulated the place in search of spirited comfort after midnight deadlines.

In an effort to accommodate the latter group, the management at McDonough's took a proactive approach to the city's problematic 2 a.m. closing time—by drawing the shades and ignoring it.

The cops didn't care, mainly because they, too, needed a decompression stop after the second shift. Besides, they had bigger fish to fry. Savannah in the late 1980s may have been middling in population, but it was in the big leagues where crime was concerned, with one of the highest murder rates in the nation. Thus did most members of the Savannah Police Department carry their weapons, concealed, when they were off duty.

It was at McDonough's that I met Glynnon Sells, a Detroit native who loved being a cop in Savannah, especially when his assignments took him to the grittier sides of town. He liked the action, so much so that he eventually left Savannah for a spot on the police force in his hometown of Detroit, reasoning that he was at the point in his career where he needed to be at ground zero of crime in the U.S.

The surest way to inflame Glynnon's dander was to call him Glynnon. He preferred Tim. In his early 30s, his curly hair had already faded from red to dull brown and was retreating from his forehead. Slight of build with wire-rimmed glasses, he looked more like a Jewish accountant than an Irish cop. To offset his unintimidating veneer, he took to talking out of the side of his mouth, like a gangster in a 1950s movie, and lacing his sentences with invectives.

One August night in 1989, with the humidity still as thick as fatback six hours after sunset, Tim and I pulled up to McDonough's simultaneously.

The front door was locked and the blinds were drawn, but the lights were ablaze. Fortunately, both of us were privy to the cunning password system.

"Charlie!" Tim shouted as he pounded on the window, "open the fucking door!"

Charlie, the bar's ex con manager, cast a wary eye through a raised slot in the blinds. The door creaked open. "You're late," he said in the same tone my mother used when dinner was getting cold. "Where are all your cronies?"

Tim shrugged his shoulders. "Ridding the streets of guys like you," he said, taking the first of what was usually a litany of good-natured digs at Charlie's vaguely criminal past.

"What about you?" Charlie said, nodding at me as if I were responsible for the dearth of newspaper employees in his establishment.

"Maybe it's that," I replied, pointing at Charlie's open ledger on the bar. Twice a month, Charlie made an attempt to square the accounts of *Savannah Morning News & Evening Press* employees, virtually all of whom ran tabs at McDonough's. Collection days tended to scare away the customers.

"Except that this isn't the normal day of reckoning," Charlie countered, showing off his latest vocabulary acquisition. Sure enough, the word-of-the-day calendar hanging above the cash register read "Reckoning."

"Goddam reporters! Do you think someone tipped them off about the new collection date?" moaned Charlie, who strayed toward paranoia when he was drinking, which was on any day ending in "y."

"Maybe it's the Jim Williams trial," I said, attempting to keep Charlie from straying to the dark side. "They acquitted him today, and everyone is busting their asses to put out special editions."

Savannah's most famous murder case had culminated earlier that day in an Augusta courtroom, several months after the defense, after years of trying, had finally succeeded in securing a change of venue. Williams, a Savannah art dealer who restored dozens of the city's historic antebellum residences to their original glory, was the only man in the history of Georgia jurisprudence to be tried four times for the same crime. After a soap opera of mistrials, convictions and appeals, Williams had finally been acquitted of the 1981 murder of his homosexual lover in Williams' famed residence, a house once occupied by Savannah native son and legendary songwriter Johnny Mercer. The eight-year saga would later be fleshed out as John Berendt's epochal bestseller, *Midnight in the Garden of Good & Evil.*

The story had been covered diligently by our paper for years. Now that it had come to a conclusion, my colleagues on the news side and in the production and press rooms were working deep into the night to put out special editions for the morning and evening papers.

"Goddamn butt pirates," Charlie said, summarizing the narrative with trademark brevity.

"You owe $27," Charlie added, swinging the ledger around in the event that I wanted to double-check his math. There was no need. I undoubtedly owed three or four times that amount, but I had the gamesmanship to order most of my drinks after Charlie started talking about his experiences in the "big house," the point at which everybody knew he was too shitfaced to engage in accurate bookkeeping.

I paid Charlie and watched as he credited my account. Then I started another tab and ordered a drink, which I nursed while waiting for the magic moment when Charlie broached the subject of his incarceration.

There were only two other people in the bar. One was Dee-Dee, whom we knew not to disturb while she was in the midst of her 3 a.m. ritual of reconciling her cash drawer, a task made exponentially more complicated by the largely illegible IOUs from newspaper employees that Charlie stuffed in the drawer at various intervals throughout the night. Dee-Dee nightly faced the task of sorting through a random collection of scribbled notes written on the backs of old receipts, corners of pages from the telephone book and, when pulp was at a premium, sheets of toilet paper.

Sitting quietly on the barstool in front of Dee-Dee was a man I hadn't seen before.

Dee-Dee paused to blow us a kiss and introduce her friend.

"Guys, this is Roshni" she said, then resumed her counting.

We exchanged hellos and some small talk, during which we discovered that Roshni was a grad student on a visa from Iran.

"Are you sleeping with her?" Charlie asked Roshni accusingly, a sure sign that he was approaching his three-sheets phase of dubious ledger maintenance.

"Charlie!" Dee-Dee screeched over the top of a stack of freshly counted bills. "Behave!"

Charlie waved her off. "You know who I slept with in the big house?" he slurred at nobody in general.

Tim took a guess. "Other guys in the big house?"

"Liftoff!" I whispered to Tim, who also knew the signal that free booze was at hand.

"C'mon, seriously," Charlie said. "Guess who I slept with in the big house?"

We were genuinely curious, given that Charlie had told us, on several occasions, that it would be front-page news if the records of his conjugal visitors were ever revealed. But he left us hanging once more. Distracted by the noise of the dishwasher, Charlie stared into the dark kitchen and then wandered off.

"Keep an eye on him," Dee-Dee said as she opened the safe behind the bar and deposited her cash and reports. "He's in rare form tonight."

"Where are you going?" Tim asked. "We want to buy you a drink."

"We all know who's buying the drinks," Dee-Dee said, pointing toward the ledger that Charlie was now too intoxicated to navigate. "But we've got to go. I'm giving Roshni a ride."

Protocol called for one of the guys in the bar to accompany Dee-Dee to her car. Tim and I had both risen for the occasion, but upon hearing that she was equipped with her own escort, I returned to my barstool.

"You sure?" Tim said, lingering in his stance.

"Completely," Dee-Dee said, giving Tim a peck on the cheek as she headed for the door with Roshni. "Lock the door behind us, hon."

"I don't know about that guy," Tim grumbled as he walked over and turned the deadbolt.

"You don't know anything about him," I replied. "He seemed nice enough."

We were trying to decide which one of us would lead the search party into the pitch-black kitchen, where Charlie was lurking, when we were jarred by urgent pounding on the door.

We looked at each other, baffled. The pounding continued, accompanied by loud and incoherent screaming.

Tim instinctively reached for his service revolver, a .38 that he kept tucked in the back of his pants. He reached behind the bar and grabbed Charlie's baseball bat and tossed it to me, then silently signaled for me to cover one side of the door while he slid into place on the opposite side. Slowly, he unbolted the lock and pushed the door open.

Dee-Dee burst into the room, sobbing hysterically, her ample bosom and derriere shaking like Jell-O on a washing machine.

Charlie suddenly reappeared and the three of us rallied around Dee-Dee, but it was more than a minute before we could get a cogent word out of her. In the meantime, Roshni slipped back into the bar unnoticed.

Dee-Dee finally gained enough composure to give us an accounting. In the 30-second walk to her car, she had been mugged. Worse yet, she was carrying more than a week's worth of tips, having failed to get to the bank in the past week. The perpetrator got away with more than $800, she estimated. That was likely to skew Dee-Dee's budget for months.

Tim tried to wring a description from her, but all she could offer was that it was a black guy.

Tim went ballistic. He ran outside and charged up and down Drayton Street, gun drawn, looking for suspects and scaring the living hell out of a group of late-night partiers from the Savannah College of Art & Design, whose students were easily identified by their hodge-podge collection of thrift-shop attire and neon hairstyles. He veered off into the park across the street, rousting the homeless black guys.

I gave up on chasing him and returned to the bar, where Dee-Dee was sobbing in Charlie's arms.

Tim followed in short order, kicking the door open in unadulterated rage after failing to collar any suspects on the street. It was then that he noticed Roshni sitting quietly at the far end of the bar, in the shadowy section near the jukebox.

"Where in the hell were you when all this was going down?" Tim screamed as he charged toward Roshni. Thankfully, he had tucked his gun away.

Dee-Dee pulled herself out of her torpor. "No!"

she yelled at Tim. "It wasn't his fault."

I jumped up to intercede, cutting off Tim's angle. "Let's find out what happened first," I suggested. Tim glared at Roshni, then nodded at me.

He returned to his seat. Charlie had disappeared into the kitchen again, so I took the opportunity to jump behind the bar to refill Tim's tumbler and pour Dee-Dee a nerve-calmer. I poured an extra beer and placed it in front of Roshni.

"Should we call someone in your division?" I asked Tim.

"Sure," he said. "Then we can figure out a story to tell my sergeant tomorrow when he asks me what I was doing in a bar at 3:30 in the morning."

"Goddamnit," Tim continued, slamming his glass on the bar. "Somebody needs to start filling in some blanks, pronto."

Dee-Dee, however, had had enough. With her mascara streaked across her face like a mutant raccoon, she told us she needed to go home. "Just a minute," Charlie said as he disappeared behind the bar. We could hear him rummaging around in the safe. As he sealed the door to the vault, Roshni stood to follow Dee-Dee out the door.

"Oh no," Charlie said as he navigated his way around the bar, holding up his arm to block Roshni's progress. "She needs a real man to walk her to her car. Sit your fuzzy ass back down, Roshelle."

With that, Charlie, who weighed about 150 pounds soaking wet, draped one arm around the considerably more substantial Dee-Dee and used the other to stuff a fat wad of bills from bar proceeds into her bra. She kissed him and began crying again. The pair headed out the door as Roshni stood there, his mouth ajar.

We knew that Dee-Dee was safe with Charlie. He loved her like a daughter and would have taken a bullet for her. He may have been a bantamweight, but he was plucky; he took shit from no man. He talked openly of prison life, but wouldn't reveal the source of his expertise, no matter how altered his state became. It was no secret that he made occasional visits to a parole officer over in Garden City. I had even given him a lift a couple of times, although he always made me drop him off a few blocks away, lest I use my reporter's wiles for financial gain.

Charlie knew all about the longstanding pool among patrons at McDonough's, where the pot was in excess of $500. It awaited anyone who could offer proof of Charlie's crime and details of his sentence. The pool's very existence seemed to fortify Charlie's will to defy it, even when all of his other systems were compromised, which was nightly.

Tim had tried working his departmental sources, but Charlie had apparently committed his crime in another jurisdiction. A few of our reporters had taken a shot, but came up empty, as well. We were pretty sure the owner of McDonough's was privy to the details, but we were also pretty sure that he was Irish Mafia, so we didn't delve too deeply. Had the Internet been available to us in the dusk of the 80s, we simply would have searched each state's department of corrections database and made cursory work of the mystery. Then again, the Pony Express would have been a lot more efficient with cargo jets.

While Charlie was escorting Dee-Dee to her car, Tim was still in interrogation mode, more irritated than ever as the minutes ticked away in his pursuit of justice.

"Looks like you're in the hot seat, Ayatollah," he

said as he transported his drink to Roshni's end of the bar.

Roshni finally spoke up, albeit in broken English. "What you call me, SAVAK?"

The Iran Hostage Crisis had ended seven years earlier, but like most Americans who endured 444 days of in-your-face news coverage as it unfolded, we were well-acquainted with SAVAK, the goon police squads that operated with impunity under the CIA-backed Shah of Iran. Tim was outraged at the insult. He charged.

Roshni stood to defend himself. Momentum conquered inertia, and the two went crashing to the floor, where they commenced to grappling. Tim got the upper hand at first, pinning Roshni's face to the floor with his forearm as he demanded an account of Roshni's whereabouts while Dee-Dee was being accosted and relieved of her cash.

I was surprised at Tim's scrappiness. Roshni, now that I could see him in the bright light of the jukebox, was a pretty well-built guy. His forearms were like cables, and Tim was having a hard time straddling his chest. I thought it best that I separated them before Tim found himself on the business end of an ass-kicking.

Charlie, who had returned from his escort duties, was of similar mind. He slurred a few largely indecipherable commands, but I was practiced enough in translating Charlie's drunk-speak to understand the gist of it: "This shit needs to stop before something gets broken."

He wasn't referring to anybody's bones. Charlie was interested only in protecting his jukebox and furnishings.

I grabbed Tim by the belt and yanked him off Roshni, pushing him in Charlie's direction. Charlie slipped his arms under Tim's armpits and thrust upward, then locked his hands behind Tim's neck to gain leverage—an old bouncer's move. I offered my hand to Roshni, who took hold as I helped him up from the floor.

He took a step toward Tim, but I simply wrapped an arm around his chest and swung him away from further confrontation. Not a thing had been broken. Yet.

Tim was trying to squirm out of Charlie's disabling grip. Charlie was once again proving to be plucky. Maybe he had learned some moves in the big house.

"Not in my bar," Charlie shouted, clamping down harder on his hold. Tim struggled for a few seconds, but Charlie's grip was firm. Tim was acquainted enough with resistance to know that it was futile in this particular hold. "I'm cool, Charlie," he said, relaxing.

I merely had my hand on Roshni's chest to create distance while I kept my eyes on Tim and Charlie. As far as I was concerned, the details of the mugging had shined a light on Roshni's disdain for confrontation. I wasn't worried about him rejoining the fight.

That's when I felt his hands on my throat.

I instinctively threw up my elbow to break the grip, but it didn't work. As his frame suggested, Roshni had some strength in reserve. My windpipe felt like it was being crushed. I threw up a knee, but since I was facing in the opposite direction, I couldn't see exactly where Roshni was positioned, and missed him entirely.

I couldn't breathe, and Tim was still under Charlie's leverage, so I knew I had to make good on the next attempt. I swung my elbow into Roshni's chest. It worked. He loosened his grip enough for me gulp down some air. I repeated the strategy, this time knocking him backwards a few steps.

I was still gasping for oxygen as I squared to face my Persian foe, still bewildered as to why I had become the focus of his wrath. I wanted nothing more than for the madness to cease and for normal programming to resume—that is, Charlie doling out drinks and forgetting to record the transactions in the ledger. "Everybody stand down," I said, rasping.

Nobody stood down. Charlie still had Tim in an arm lock. Like the Energizer Bunny, Roshni just kept coming at me.

So I hit him, a right cross that landed squarely on his nose. He fell backwards into a table, breaking a couple of chairs on the way down. There was blood everywhere, including a splatter pattern on my K-Mart designer button-down shirt, which I had purchased just a day earlier.

Until that point, I had merely been defending myself. Now I was pissed. "Dammit" I said as I unbuttoned the shirt and folded it neatly over the jukebox. "You're going to pay for that, Ayatollah! Get up so I can hit you again!"

Then I heard the click.

With Tim's arms hiked above his head in Charlie's death grip, his shirt had risen to reveal the .38 he kept tucked in his waistline. When Charlie saw the chairs splinter, he simply reached down and grabbed the revolver, then threw Tim backwards over his outstretched leg, knocking him to the floor. As I was finishing removing my shirt to prevent any further breach of fashion, Charlie walked up behind me, stuck the gun to my temple and cocked the trigger.

Time stopped. But Charlie's slurry voice cut through the haze like a foghorn.

"You want to destroy my barroom," he said. "Then let's see what this bullet does to your brain."

Charlie's breath smelled like a dog's ass. But I understood every syllable.

"What the fuck, Charlie," I heard Tim yell from the floor, "I'll pay for the chairs, man. That's Brian! He's your friend, you fucking nutjob!"

Although I deemed this an inopportune moment for Tim to be insulting Charlie, I was glad to have an ally at my execution. I reiterated Tim's theme.

"Charlie, it's me … Brian!" I said. "I drove you to your parole officer last month! We stopped for ice cream!"

Charlie failed to react. His eyes were glazed and evil lurked within. I had a chilling thought: Charlie wanted to go back to prison. And I would be his conduit.

I closed my eyes, determined to make my peace in the moments I had remaining. Instead, I became fixated on the fact that I was about to die without a shirt. Charlie would probably kill Tim, too, and frame him, posthumously, with his own gun. There we'd lie, side by side, me half-clothed, at 4 a.m. The detectives would surely brand it a murder-suicide between lovers.

Considering Tim's profession and my flirtation with fame, it would be national news. I could see the tabloid headlines: "Romeo and Julius" or "Til Death Do Them Part." My parents would be devastated. "Surely there was some mistake—he always seemed so into women," they'd say as their friends nodded in sympathy and whispered among themselves. "Come to think of it, he always did seem preoccupied," my former girlfriends would say. And on and on, until I was right up there with Noel Coward or T.S. Elliott in my allegiance to the cause.

Why couldn't my life just flash before me, like a normally wired human?

I wasn't sure how much time had passed, but I didn't seem to be dead. I opened one eye. There, filling up the view, was Roshni's face. He had decided to seize the moment—by seizing my throat once again.

To put it mildly, I wasn't very excited about my options: death by choking or by lead poisoning of the cerebral cortex. I decided to take one last stab at diplomatic intervention.

"Charlie," I pleaded, my voice hoarse from the larynx abuse, "tell him to back off or I'm gonna hit him again."

At last, I elicited a response from Charlie. "Go ahead," he said as he nuzzled the gun a bit more firmly into my temple. "Throw another punch."

With all roads leading to nowhere, I decided to take Charlie's advice. I punched Roshni with all the strength I could muster. Then I closed my eyes for my reckoning.

I heard a lot of crashing. I was pretty sure the Pearly Gates wouldn't be that noisy. Hell, on the other hand ...

I opened my eyes to find both Roshni and Charlie on the floor. Roshni was lying prone on the same table he had broken moments earlier. Charlie was looking up at the .38 that was now pointed at him, trying to figure out how Tim had turned the tables so quickly.

"Freeze, assholes," Tim said with a smirk.

It took about 15 minutes to get things sorted out. Tim directed Charlie to a barstool and handcuffed one of his wrists to the arched brass fixture that delineated the waitress station from the rest of the bar. But he took mercy and poured a scotch, which Charlie tossed back with his free hand.

Tim walked over and pointed the gun at Roshni. "Clean it up" he said, throwing a bar rag at his head. Roshni set to work mopping up his blood, which was splattered on the walls and had, in places, pooled on the floor.

"Somebody's going to pay for all that damage," Charlie slurred from the bar.

Tim walked over to the bar and turned the gun around, grabbing it by the barrel. In a violent motion, he slammed the grip down on Charlie's scotch glass, shattering it. "That's your face, the next time you open your mouth," said Tim, who had reclaimed his identity as a cop—and a rightfully outraged one at that.

The diversion was all that Roshni needed. He bolted for the door, never to be seen again. Tim took a few indecisive steps, as if he was considering giving chase, but I cut him off. "Let him go," I pleaded, having been drained of all the adrenaline that further confrontation would have required. "We're never going to find the guy who mugged Dee-Dee."

Tim returned to the bar. I walked into the kitchen, flicked on the light and looked in the mirror. My neck was already discolored from Roshni's strangulation attempts. Purple-and-black bruises would form in the next day or so. Fuck. I hated turtlenecks. I wasn't even sure that one had made the trip with me from Ohio.

I found the mop bucket. Rooting around, I located some bleach and a pair of rubber gloves. I filled the bucket and wheeled it into the bar.

The mood had drastically changed. Charlie and Tim were sharing a laugh as Tim reeled off a list of holy grievances that would have befallen him at the office had Charlie killed me with a police-issue firearm. "I'd have been buried up to my ass in paperwork," Tim said out of the side of his mouth, neglecting to note that I would have been buried up to my ass in cemetery dirt. A bottle of Glenlivet sat between them. Charlie's eyes were bloodshot, as if he'd been crying. Charlie poured Tim a drink with his free hand. I stared in disbelief as Tim reached into his pocket and produced the key to the handcuffs, setting Charlie free.

Charlie rubbed his wrist and took another swig. Then he stood up and headed in my direction. Instinctively, I threw up my hands. "Back off, Charlie, you psychopath."

"Awww, come on," Charlie said, his arms open wide and his eyes filling with tears. He threw his arms wildly around my neck, as if he was trying to gather in the greased pig at the county fair.

"Brian, my friend," he said, his dog's ass breath making me nauseous. "I am so sorry. Can you forgive your buddy, Charlie? I get a little crazy-wazy sometimes."

I knew it was the alcohol talking. Charlie probably wouldn't remember a single detail the next day. I felt badly for him. His had been a hard road.

"No worries, Charlie," I said, returning a half-assed, one-armed hug, as much compassion as I could muster for my would-be assassin. "But the rounds are on you until hell freezes over."

Charlie laughed, baring his rotting teeth and giving me another whiff of the bowels of his intestines. "Thatta boy," he said, patting me on my ass. "Jack Sandwiches on the house!"

Charlie grabbed my shirt from the jukebox and took it behind the bar with him. He dropped it in a bus tub, then grabbed the soda gun and began filling it with club soda. "Here's a little housekeeping tip from your ol' buddy Charlie" he said with a rot-tooth grin.

Sure enough, all the blood eventually leeched out of my shirt. Remarkably, Charlie had been transformed from Charles Manson to Martha Stewart. Now, if we could just find some industrial-strength mouthwash …

As my shirt was soaking, I set about putting the room in order. I gathered the broken pieces of table and chair and swept them into the pile. I bleached down the floor and mopped up the blood that Roshni had missed, then wiped the walls clean of the DNA evidence of our little soiree. I dragged the biggest pieces of wood to the dumpster and piled the rest in boxes, which I also transported out back. I even rearranged the garbage to make sure the evidence wasn't hovering in plain sight at the top of the dumpster when the bar's owner pulled into his parking space around lunchtime.

By the time I finished, the sun was casting its first rays over the horizon.

Charlie was asleep at a corner table when I returned. Tim was on the pay phone with his stationhouse, checking to see if anyone had been apprehended in the historic district with $800 or so. He hung up, disappointed.

It was fully morning when we collected our things to leave. We roused Charlie so he could lock up. The three of us decided to walk. Tim and Charlie lived close, and although I was several miles away, I decided that some Georgia sunshine would do my club soda-drenched shirt a world of good.

As we were walking out the door, we passed the conspicuously empty spot near the jukebox where the now-decimated table and chairs had stood.

"Listen, Charlie," I said, reaching into my pocket for any stray cash. "I don't want you to take heat for the furniture I broke. How much to replace everything?"

He waved me off.

"Oh, don't worry about that," he said as he filed through his voluminous key chain in an attempt to lock up. "We're re-doing the whole place next week with new tables and chairs."

In the wretched heat of south Georgia, my shirt was dry before I walked a mile. But another mile in it had been thoroughly re-soaked by sweat, so I took it off for home stretch to my apartment. The hard sun illuminated my life, and I grimaced at what was laid bare. I had come precariously close to death. The realization filled me with consternation.

As I examined my shirt in the harsh light, I discovered that the club soda had only lightened the blood stains, but not eradicated them. As I approached a trash can in the parking lot of an auto parts store to discard the shirt, panic born of the reality of that night's events rose from my stomach into my throat. I deposited the shirt into the bin … then vomited on top of it.

I needed to make some changes.

9

Farewell, My Lovely

I followed up the Evans-Effingham County story with a local blockbuster the following football season, when I discovered the coach at Savannah High—a man I admired and to whom I had presented our newspaper's Chatham County coach of the year award a few months earlier—was conducting illegal practice sessions before the preseason opened. I just happened to be driving by the school and couldn't believe they were practicing right out in the open, with no pretense of subterfuge.

When I parked and approached him, he claimed to be unaware of the state-mandated opening-day for preseason camp. He lowered his head in shame. Then he looked me in the eye and implored me not to write anything. I could see that his desperation was real. Fuck. Objective reporting, my ass. Everything was subjective. I'd figured that out just three years out of journalism school. But there was no decision to be made.

I went into a meditative state and summoned

another version of myself, the one that was necessary to deploy when I had to do something way out of my comfort zone, be it jumping from a plane, defending myself from a physical threat, or asking an interview subject a hard question. I even had a name for that persona: Disconnected Brian. It was Disconnected Brian that got me up the death-defying cables of Yosemite Park's Half Dome two decades later, and pulled me out of more than a few wilderness settings after I'd become lost.

I, Brian, wanted to invite the desperate coach in front for a beer. But Disconnected Brian had been called to pinch-hit. He simply leveled his gaze and calmly said, "I can't do that, coach. I wouldn't be doing my job." Disconnected Brian turned on his heels and walked in a measured pace back to the car. When he got there, he handed the reins back. Brian fumbled for his keys, dropping them on the pavement twice before managing to open the door.

Like his counterpart at Evans High, the Savannah coach's career came to an abrupt halt. Perhaps fearing that further media exploration would reveal the kind of systemic allergy to rules that was diagnosed at Evans, the school district went a step further, firing Savannah High's principal and athletic director, as well. There were a few accusations of racism from the community toward our paper—the coach was black, as were a preponderance of Savannah High's students—but those charges lost momentum when a local TV station ran a story about all the people who lost their livelihoods as a result of my reporting in the past year (there had been some residual fallout among administrators in Augusta, as well). All but one was white.

About the same time, I wrote a story about a football player in rural Screven County who had been killed in a car crash at the outset of his senior year. I remember driving down a dirt road to a corrugated shack to interview his relatives, who went out of their way to make me feel welcome—and, of course, well fed—in their time of unfathomable grief. There were high hopes, before the tragedy, that the young athlete would escape the abject poverty of this unpaved road without a name, one that white folks like me seldom traveled.

The latter story won an *Associated Press* story of the year award for high school sports, making me the first writer from the Savannah paper to win *AP* first-place awards in consecutive years in nearly half a century. Once again, however, the paper refused to foot the bill for the awards banquet in Atlanta.

Determined by my near-death experience to make changes where changes availed themselves as prudent, I circled my second anniversary with the paper as my final day and submitted my notice.

It was a lose-lose situation. I didn't want to leave, but felt grossly undercompensated in light of my performance. My editors didn't want to lose me, but were hamstrung by the cheap bastard who owned the chain. I wrote a heart-felt (and heartbroken) exit column, which our opinion-page editor adorned with a headline so graceful that I still get misty-eyed when I spot it in my files. With a tip of the hat to detective novelist Raymond Chandler, it read, simply, "Farewell, My Lovely."

A few weeks later, with my resignation date behind me, I felt like a character in a Raymond Chandler novel as I sat in the lobby of the Mulberry Inn, a throwback to a more elegant era. At the time of day when most places are cranking up their happy hours, the Mulberry served complimentary tea while a jazz aficionado tickled the ivories in the piano lounge.

Although the Mulberry and the *Savannah Morning News & Evening Press* were located just two blocks apart on Bay Street, I had never stepped foot in the place until getting a call one day from the property's new manager. He had a proposition and invited me to stop by to hear it.

I had yet to figure out my next move. If I wanted to continue on a journalism arc—and I was sure I did—I would have to leave town. So why hadn't I? I had parlayed all my plaudits into exactly nothing, and every day I spent in Savannah meant more lichen growing on my byline.

Wearing the only pair of pants I owned with a crease, I stepped into the Mulberry's world of privilege feeling like a dandelion among the lilies. I was as befuddled as I was unemployed.

The manager of the Mulberry, being steeped in Southern hospitality, greeted me with a invitation to imbibe. "Let's talk in the lounge," he said. We adjourned to an impressive room of hand-carved dark oak and polished brass.

"Have you ever been in here?" he asked.

"I'm sorry to say that I haven't," I replied. "My loss. It's a beautiful room."

"But not the kind of place where you and your friends might hang out?" he countered.

"Well," I said, trying to figure his angle, "we rotate the nice pair of pants among ourselves, so we can only go in places like this one at a time. I just lucked out that it was my turn today."

He chuckled. "That's exactly the kind of

perception I'm trying to change," he said.

A waitress arrived with two drinks. "Scotch on the rocks," she said, placing one in front of the boss. "And for you, sir, a Jack Sandwich."

I raised my eyebrows. "I'm impressed," I said, toasting my host.

"I talked to my share of bartenders on River Street when I took this job," he said.

The manager pointed to a table of blue-haired ladies sipping on Vermouth-based drinks. "I'd like to get a fresher crowd in here," he said.

His idea: to start a sports trivia night two days a week. He had done his due diligence by calling my former editor and by talking to River Street tavern owners, in search of the ideal host for such an undertaking.

"The consensus was that if I was looking to lower the property value," he said, "you were the guy to hire."

So that's what I did for the next few months, filling in the gaps by working bar shifts that paid nearly double what I made as a reporter two blocks away. But as I suspected from the outset, the trivia nights were a poor fit for the venue. The Mulberry was no more a sports bar than I was a four-star hotel employee.

One night, in an effort to help me promote the doomed program, the sports anchor from one of Savannah's TV stations showed up to do a story on our sports trivia nights. I rushed home to watch his report on the 11 o'clock news. I was mortified to see my bloated figure on the screen. I had arrived in town in the best shape of my life, but gone soft as I succumbed to the prurient pleasures of being a public figure in this sultry, seductive antebellum city.

I was a poor man's Jim Williams, the protagonist in *Midnight in the Garden of Good and Evil.* Bad things awaited me if I stayed.

10

Texas Hexes

I picked up the pieces of my incremental journalism career by returning to Phoenix for a few years. Unlike the tarred rooftops on which I earned a meager paycheck a half-dozen years earlier, however, the offices of the *Phoenix Gazette* were air-conditioned. But the Gazette itself was on life support, a common fate among afternoon publications in two-paper markets during the 1980s and '90s.

Years later, when I was conducting public relations for an observatory and planetarium in the trail-laced Oakland hills, one of the astronomers confided that his dream was to see a supernova in his lifetime. It had been more than 500 years since one had lit up the Milky Way Galaxy.

But for those of us who experienced the transition of journalism from a hard-copy industry to a digital one, supernovas were all around. They were called Joint Operating Agreements (JOAs). In its death throes, a once-mighty newspaper—predominantly the afternoon newspapers in a two-paper market—would glom onto a thriving paper, suck off just enough energy to raise its core temperature to create the illusion of fusion, then explode spectacularly before fading to black.

The *Gazette* was doomed. I didn't wait for the fireworks in Phoenix. After a two-year hitch in my second deployment in the desert, I traded Phoenix for another version of meteorological hell. Hello, Texas!

I relocated with the promise of some freelance work by the *Fort Worth Star-Telegram*'s assistant sports editor, Scott Monserud, who had hired me at the *Southern Illinoisan* nine years earlier. I slept on Scott's couch for a few weeks, but he had a wife and a young daughter, so I traded those accommodations for a transient motel located, like much of Texas, near a topless bar.

Eventually, the glamour of toothless neighbors pounding 40-ounce malt liquors and the 2 a.m. awakenings by insurance salesmen coming to orgasm at the hands of haggardly 30-year-old strippers wore off, and I began to look around for a more dignified address.

Scott came through with journalism assignments. I wrote several articles a week about the colleges nobody cared about, the University of Texas-Arlington and the University of North Texas. I supplemented my income stream when the owner of the topless bar saw me pulling into the motel one night and asked me if I'd be interested in bouncing a few nights a week at another of his establishments across town.

Contrary to what one might think about employment at a place where young women remove their clothes as part of their job description, it's not exactly titillating work. Soon enough, it became too depressing to tolerate. The manager was a slime-bag and far too many of the girls—who were supposed to be a minimum of 18 years old—spent their time between stage appearances chain smoking and fantasizing about the day they would graduate high school.

The Cavalry arrived just in time. The Fort Worth Cavalry was a fledgling team in the Arena Football League. In other words, another sports team that nobody gave a shit about. Naturally, that fell into my job description. In Texas, arena football ranked a few orbits below high school football. No self-respecting sports editor wanted to waste any of his salaried employees' time on such nonsense. I was happy to have the work covering the team for the *Star-Telegram*.

The Cavalry lasted just one season, but the extra income allowed me to retire from the breast-showcasing business. No matter. There were plenty of breasts—all of them attached to women of legal voting age—at the invitation-only rooftop parties in downtown Fort Worth thrown by the team after every game. I became particularly attached to the near-perfect, non-surgically altered ones belonging to the Cavalry's bleached-blonde media relations coordinator who, at 24, was eight years my junior.

She was so stunning that I could easily count, as we walked through any restaurant, a half-dozen gaping jaws belonging to men who were dining with their own wives or girlfriends. She was, understandably, hated by other women. But she was wholly uninterested in countering their venom with any niceties; she didn't see the point in wasting time courting favors with a gender that she wholeheartedly believed was populating the planet merely as support staff.

Behind my back (so they thought), my friends named her "The Biscuit," ostensibly for her butter-melting qualities.

By the time I got caught in her tractor beam, I had upgraded to a third-story apartment midway between Dallas and Fort Worth, overlooking a massive construction site. Beam by beam, I watched the Ballpark at Arlington, home of the Texas Rangers, take form.

There were signs that I was out of my league with The Biscuit. One day, she inspected my CD collection and promptly proclaimed: "You have some decent music here, but you'll never get laid in Texas with this collection."

"Ummm, I was under the impression that I was getting laid," I replied.

She laughed, although a man with more common sense would have heard a serpent's hiss. "It's a phase, sweetie," she replied. "You should be prepared for the next one. Get some country music."

Shortly after I met her, one of the *Star-Telegram*'s news-side reporters wrote a story about some suspected financial malfeasance at a local high school. Because one of the people suspected of shenanigans served the dual role of the school's athletic director and football coach, the sports department was enlisted to help flesh out the details. But our high school beat writers were stonewalled by their usual contacts and couldn't get anywhere with the story.

Scott knew all about my history in Georgia, so he asked me to dig around a bit. The Biscuit pointed me toward a few of the Cavalry players who knew of the coach from their high school playing days. I slipped his name into the conversation at one of the post-game bashes on the roof, then just sat back and listened. Their sordid tales began flowing in pace with the booze. The next thing I knew, I was writing front-page stories and the athletic director/coach was looking for work. My kill list was beginning to resemble Billy The Kid's.

At about the same time, two legendary Dallas Cowboys, Tony Dorsett and Randy White, were being inducted into the Pro Football Hall of Fame. Although I grew up in Ohio, I was a hardcore Cowboys' fan as a kid. Knowing that, the *Star-Telegram*'s executive sports editor, Kevin Dale (Scott's boss), threw me a bone and assigned me to write Hall of Fame induction stories for both players.

I spent one of the coolest days of my career hanging out with Dorsett at his North Dallas house and then at his tailor's shop, where he was being fitted for his Hall of Fame induction suit. That evening, I met White at his favorite restaurant, a hole-in-the-wall Mexican joint in Fort Worth, and interviewed him over dinner. As a stringer, I still wasn't making much money. I remember taking every last dollar from my checking account and still being nervous that I wasn't going to have enough to pay the nominal bill at the Mexican place, which only accepted cash.

I didn't know it at the time, but I was auditioning. The paper had two full-time Cowboys beat writers and a third staffer who covered the rest of the NFL as it pertained to the Cowboys. The NFL writer was having some issues with Kevin and was looking around for a new gig. He soon found one in Houston.

When the opening became official, I begged Kevin for a shot. He had already lined up a few reporters to interview, but acknowledged that I had been a loyal and productive grunt in a freelance role. All he could promise, he said, was a date on his interview calendar.

That's when The Biscuit took over.

"When is your next softball game?" she asked,

showing the first modicum of interest in my role as one of the *Star-Telegram*'s outfielders.

"Sunday," I replied. "Since when have you cared?"

"Will your editors be there?" she asked.

"Probably," I said. "They're on the team."

"Well, I'm coming with you," she declared.

She sat behind the fence, three rows up from home plate, where her perfectly tanned legs, perfectly sculpted body and angelic face gave immense pleasure to every player on both teams for seven innings. She cheered me on the entire game, even when I misjudged the wall on a home run and bounced off the chain-link fence like Wile E. Coyote. We lost, as usual, but in the last inning I hit a meaningless inside-the-park homer, sliding head-first across the plate just ahead of the tag. The dugout, having little else to cheer about, erupted.

As we were walking off the field following the final out a few minutes later, The Biscuit held back and waited until I was engaged in conversation with some of the editors from various departments. She strategically interrupted by running up behind me and grabbing my ass, which was totally out of character for her.

"Nice hit, stud," she said, and kissed me on the lips. "We need to get you home and properly cleaned up for dinner." Again, words I had never heard flow from her lips.

The editors just stood there, as dazed as I was. "Lucky S.O.B." I heard one of them mutter as I followed her to the car. As I was putting the keys in the ignition, The Biscuit slapped me on the knee.

"See that!" she said, grinning from ear to ear. "That's how we close business here. That job is yours!"

Kevin hired me a few days later, just a few hours after my interview.

I wasn't very good at the job, in part because I started just as the season began and was totally unconnected in the NFL—and in part because I was going through a shitty phase as a writer. Looking back on old newspaper clips, I was a much more inspired wordsmith at my ensuing gig, covering college football for the *Oakland Tribune*. But, as with The Biscuit, I thoroughly enjoyed the ride. That's because 1994 was the best season in the history of the *Star-Telegram* to be the NFL writer.

Normally, the beat largely would have been conducted on the phone, calling general managers and participating in scheduled teleconferences with players and coaches, as well as focusing on the visiting locker room at Cowboys home games. But that year was unprecedented in the annals of sport, with both Major League Baseball players and National Hockey League players on strike. The significant money that the newspaper had budgeted for reporters covering the Texas Rangers and Dallas Stars was diverted into the NFL budget—which meant that I got to travel, constantly. The Cowboys are playing the Browns next week? Let's send Brian to Cleveland to write some feature stories! The New York Giants are on the Cowboys' schedule? Let's send Brian to the Big Apple to cover the Giants-Lions game!

We were so flush with funds in 1994 that Kevin once called me into his office to have the following discussion:

Kevin: "Come in, Brian. I was just looking over your last expense report."

Me: "Oh shit. Did I screw up the math somewhere?"

A GOOD LOOK BEFORE DARK

Kevin: "No, nothing like that. I've gotta say, for a guy with the sloppiest desk in the newsroom, you have the most meticulous expense reports I've ever seen."

Me: "Well, you have to choose your battles."

Kevin: "So the topic of the day is 'restaurant receipts.'"

Me: (Gulp)

Kevin: "Do you ever drink on the road?"

Me: "Umm, yeah, sure. You know me. I enjoy the occasional cocktail."

Kevin: "Uh-huh. Occasional. That's a good one. Anyway, I don't see any alcohol charges on your receipts."

Me: "What? I would never bill the paper for that!" (Like most reporters, I padded my meal expenses to cover booze).

Kevin: "Well, that's the problem. I have to show that I've spent every penny of my budget at the end of the month. Start expensing that stuff. Your alcohol budget should drain most of my overage."

The keys to the kingdom, at long last, were mine.

I took full advantage of the policy at the Super Bowl in Miami at the end of that season. I was hanging out with my buddy and former colleague, Don Ketchum of the *Arizona Republic*, at 3.30 a.m. We were glued to a couple of stools at an outdoor bar in South Beach when I began to fret that I hadn't spent enough money on booze that day. I was out of cash, however, and didn't want to burden our bartender by opening a tab so close to closing time. "It's okay," the barkeep assured me, "but there's a minimum of $25 on credit cards." He had just announced last call, meaning that we'd have to surrender any unfinished alcohol in 15 minutes. I looked at Don. "I have to be up in four hours for an interview," he said, shaking his head. "I'm only good for one or two more."

I paused but momentarily. "Alright, let's do it," I said, and handed the credit card to the bartender.

We were just a few sips in when a long-haired, deeply tanned Sicilian girl from the Jersey Shore walked by on the sidewalk, accompanied by her far less remarkable friend.

I've always been a firm believer that pickup lines are for losers. An optimistic "Hello" is far and away the most effective salutation when meeting a woman. But fate had presented me with the perfect opening gambit, and I took it.

"You're not going to believe this," I said, tapping the open bar stool next to me, "but we have to put several more drinks on our tab before closing time. Would you mind helping us out?"

That's how I met Arlene, a woman whom I would date briefly but come to love as a treasured friend for life.

The San Francisco 49ers won the Super Bowl by 23 points over the San Diego Chargers, the same margin by which they'd beat the Chargers in San Diego six weeks earlier. I covered both games, as well as many other 49ers games, because they were considered the Cowboys' chief rival for NFL supremacy.

The first time I flew back from California that season, I thought, "It's kind of a bummer having to return to Texas." Several trips later, after The Biscuit had mulched me and moved on to greener pastures (gifting me with a CD of Garth Brooks' greatest hits on her way out the door), my reticence had evolved into "I can't believe I have to go back to that damn prairie."

I'm fond of saying that the paper's budget that year was the temptress that lured me to California, like your girlfriend introducing you to your next girlfriend. But the truth is that the divorce was mutual—and I wasn't originally pointed west.

There was one last pile of mad money remaining in the budget before things returned to normal in 1995, with baseball and hockey players going back to work. Kevin used it to send me to the football owners' meeting in Phoenix, where I screwed up the final tally on the vote to allow the Los Angeles Rams to move to St. Louis. Kevin, who had become as irritated with me as he had with my predecessor, was furious.

I had some vacation time coming after the long season and wasn't planning on returning right away directly to Texas. Instead, I had a rendezvous with Arlene, the temptress I met at the Super Bowl in Miami. We were booked for a week in my parents' condo in Destin—one of the many towns along the Gulf of Mexico on Florida's panhandle that collectively form the "Redneck Riviera." My parents had owned the beachfront property for a decade and I had never laid eyes on the place. I figured it was a good time to make myself scarce. Kevin needed time to decompress.

Arlene and I spent the week mostly huddled inside waiting out a hellacious storm that relented only briefly during our stay. On one such occasion, we took advantage of the respite by driving down the coast. When we returned a few days later, the unobstructed view of the gulf from our balcony was all but totally obstructed by the framing for a new restaurant on the beach. My dad's reaction upon hearing that bit of news transported me back to my college days, when Scott found me crashed in his bed after a 15-mile trek from my gas-starved car.

It rained again the next day, our last in town. I returned to Texas, thoroughly defeated.

The hatchet dropped on my first day back. Kevin reassigned me to the high school bureau in Arlington, where my job pretty much became writing stories about a lanky, pimply, introverted kid at Grand Prairie South High School who could throw a 96 m.p.h. fastball. Kerry Wood was the first high school player taken in that year's Major League Baseball draft. He rose to instant fame by striking out a major-league record-tying 20 batters in a game in his debut season with the Chicago Cubs, when he was named National League Rookie of the Year.

On draft day, I was hanging out in the Wood's living room in Irving with Kerry and his parents, Gerry and Terry, when I decided that my life no longer had any rhyme in the Dallas-Fort Worth Metroplex. A kid half my age was about to earn more money on a signing bonus than I'd ever seen, and though I didn't begrudge him a cent, Texas had worn me thin. I had at the ready a pile of 8 x 11 envelopes containing résumés and newspaper clips—half bound for San Francisco Bay Area papers, the other for New York-area papers. I decided to let fate dictate my direction; if Kerry was drafted by a team east of the Mississippi River, I'd focus my job-hunting in the New York area, where I had accrued some connections. If not, I'd zero in on California.

Kerry's draft party was still in its first hour when the Cubs made short work of the drama. I shook hands with Gerry, Terry and Kerry, wished them luck, and told them I was leaving the paper. I've always subscribed to the theory that the first thing you should do when making a big decision is to tell somebody. It may not have been written in stone, but my resolution was now forged in three different types of Wood.

A GOOD LOOK BEFORE DARK

I still had some vacation time, so before word of my demotion got around, I lined up interviews with four New York-area papers. They were happy to talk to me, especially since it didn't cost them a dime. Using Arlene's house in the Jersey Shore town of Belmar as my launching pad, I went about securing new employment.

The interview with the *Newark Star-Ledger* seemed promising, but when I called to check on the hiring progress, I learned that the editor who had interviewed me had been fired (presumably for something other than interviewing me). Two other interviews, with *Newsday* and the *Bergen (N.J.) Record* were pleasant enough, but neither paper had an immediate opening.

All of those dead-end talks, however, were Gettysburg Addresses compared to my interview with *The New York Times*.

On the biggest stage a journalist can ever hope to set foot upon, I tightened up like a drum. At one point, when asked to list some of my favorite *Times'* sports writers, I couldn't remember the name of a single staffer.

Having once again heard the universe loud and clear, I turned my attention toward California, where I really longed to be. Without bothering to secure a job, I bid Texas adieu.

On Aug. 6, 1995, 50 years to the day after the first atomic bomb landed on the island city of Hiroshima, Japan, I landed on the island city of Alameda in San Francisco Bay.

Relocation offered me the opportunity to further bond with my close friend of 15 years. Scott Davis, my co-pilot in the Ghetto Cruiser, had abandoned a promising business career to learn how to fly airplanes.

He was teaching at Sierra Academy, a school for pilots at Oakland International Airport, and stacking up as much flight time as he could in pursuit of the 1,500 hours necessary to obtain his airline transport pilot certificate. I came along for the ride whenever possible.

In that pre-9/11 world, the only thing Scott enjoyed more than practicing aerobatics over San Francisco Bay was practicing aerobatics with an unsuspecting passenger on board.

Rising out of the bayside Oakland airport one day, he wasted no time in implementing that day's antics. "Hey, remember that piece of shit Ghetto Cruiser?" he asked as we ascended to altitude. "Uh-huh," I answered, figuring I was in for another exaggerated recounting of the day he walked 170 miles across the Northern Illinois desert after Kip and I deserted him. "You know what I remember about the Ghetto Cruiser?" he added, oblivious to my end of the conversation. "I remember how it stalled … like this."

With that, Scott pulled full aft on the yolk until our tiny plane lost lift, plunging toward the bay.

There's no telling how long he had waited to put me in that precise situation and pull that gag, but he was profoundly disappointed with the results. After he casually restarted the plane and the color returned to my face, I squealed with glee, as I had as a child when our father threw all of us kids into a pile on the bed and tickled us until somebody peed. I begged Scott to let me take control of the stick until he relented, then I aimed the plane upward until I was able to put it into a stall. Not being a pilot, I got a sensation from the ordeal that Scott did not—vertigo. I remember being surprised that one could induce this level of disorientation naturally, with nary a drink or chemical in the mix.

Scott informed me that one's tolerance to the thrills builds pretty quickly. And it was true. Our stalling exercises—legitimate training for an up-and-coming pilot, but one that the preponderance of his students hated—not only ruined me for life for roller coasters, but soon left me hankering for more horseplay in the heavens.

That's when Scott upped the ante and introduced me to a practice that he didn't even share with his student pilots: pulling out of a spin. By inputting full left or right rudder, you could make the plane fall out of the sky and rotate like a top at the same time. It was absolutely terrifying the first few times, but ours had long been a friendship whereby trust was implicit, even at the level of releasing ultimate control—that of our lives—into the hands of the other.

But after having had my stomach turned inside out a few times on each excursion, we settled into a routine whereby Scott would fly along the eastern or western edge of the bay and we'd enjoy the grandeur in the silence of old friends, he looking for telltale cloud formations and me staring, longingly, at the hillside trails below, promising myself that I would learn not only the names but the intimate twists and turn of each one.

It turns out the only thing I wanted more than the acquisition of adrenaline was the absolute abatement of it, which I eventually came to find in those hills.

I settled in, trading the placeholder bartending gig I secured a few weeks after my arrival for a corporate writing job. No sooner was I living the good life in California however, than journalism came calling again. I had kept in touch with many of the Bay Area sportswriters I'd met during all those long encampments from Texas. One of them, Don Coulter, the sports editor for the *Oakland Tribune*, invited me to lunch one day and offered me a job as the paper's lead college football writer on the spot. The money didn't come close to the salary I was making in the corporate world, so he told me to sleep on it. He wanted a decision within 48 hours.

There wasn't much to think about, really. Baptized by the gospel according to Woody Hayes in Columbus, Ohio, college football had always been my first love. The University of California-Berkeley Golden Bears sucked, but that wasn't a bad thing for a journalist: there's much more drama with bad teams than with mediocre ones. And I had never been motivated by money, despite trying endlessly to be.

I was all in.

11

The Longest Day

Being a college football writer, I had the best gig at the paper. My season didn't drag on endlessly like the pro sports. Travel, generally to other scenic West Coast locations, was easy. During college football season, it was rare for me to have a complete day off, but that was fine by me. By the time burnout set in toward the end of each season, I had accumulated so much comp time that the first few months of each year were like extended vacations.

Not that I even bothered tracking it—Jon Becker, who had succeeded New England-bound Don Coulter as sports editor a few years after I was hired, was a great boss. During the off-season, it was rare for Jon to press me into service more than two or three times a week, and then it was interesting work, filling in for one of the other beat writers to cover the Oakland A's, San Francisco Giants or Golden State Warriors.

As a beat writer, my work days were spent at ballparks and on practice fields. I rarely had to go into the office. But every three months or so, Jon would

115

gather his sports staff of 40 or so for an in-house meeting. It was on May 1, 2002 that we learned of the foreboding future of the *Oakland Tribune*, with budget and personnel cuts looming. It was the same meeting held in every department of every newspaper in the country within a few years of the turn of the millennium. The supernova was underway.

Newspapers, whose income had traditionally derived from advertising, couldn't compete with the emergence of online classified ads and job boards. Our May Day meeting made it clear that the ship was sinking. My job wasn't in jeopardy, but the nature of it was. Although it would be a while before I had to deal with the issue, beat writers like me were soon to have all that off-season down time severely compromised by filling in the ever-growing gaps among copy editors. The turnover among that group was little better than fast-food restaurant employees. Instead of hiring new ones when they quit, our newspaper chain filled in the gaps by forcing all those salaried beat writers to come into the office during their off-seasons and work eight-hour shifts editing other writers' copy. It was akin to handing an architect a tool belt and telling him to get busy nailing the beams.

During the meeting, Jon somehow picked up on a vibe that I was opposed to the idea, likely because I shouted "No fucking way!" when the subject was broached. In a one-on-one session after the meeting, he assured me that it wouldn't take effect, in my case, until the upcoming football season, my sixth with the paper, ended in January 2003. So I had eight months to get used to the idea. I assured him that time wouldn't change my temperament. "Well," he said, "don't sweat it right now. You have tomorrow off. Relax."

I went home. But I didn't relax. I was trying to put a feature story to bed so that I could enjoy a guilt-free day off on May 2 when someone knocked on my door. "Come in" I shouted, but Ike had already burst into the kitchen.

"Higgy," my somnambulant friend said with uncharacteristic urgency, employing a nickname that only friends from college knew, "can you call 911?"

"Where's the fire?" I inquired.

"In my ass. I just shit blood."

From any other human being on the planet, I'd have been fumbling for the phone. But Ike had a special relationship with that particular turn of phrase. As classmates at DePaul University three decades earlier, Ike was renowned for igniting the fire under any provocation for drinking by invoking a graphic catch phrase that was entirely of his own creation: "Party 'til you shit blood!"

"C'mon, man," I groused. "I want to finish this story tonight. Go shit blood in your own apartment."

"I already did," he replied, "and then again outside your building."

With that, he turned around to reveal the blood-stained seat of his pants. It looked as though he'd sat on a grenade.

"Whoa!" I blurted out in repulsion and panic. "What the … how did that … fuck, Ike!"

Ike and I had been casual friends for most of my two years at DePaul, but we cemented the relationship as roommates at spring break in Daytona Beach, Fla. late in our sophomore year. I didn't have much contact with him after I transferred to Southern Illinois to pursue a journalism degree, but his circle of friends intersected mine, and it was as if 15 years had been but a few months when we re-connected at the funeral of

Scott's mother in Chicago in 1998.

Tall, bespectacled and pear-shaped (even in college), Ike—the youngest of three sons of Polish immigrants—was never much of a ladies' man. After a long-term college relationship with a buck-toothed Irish girl went south, he threw in the towel. After graduating, he consented to marry a pretty Filipina for $2,000, a sum that the bride's brothers promised to double after two years, following a pre-planned divorce. By that time, his bride would be in possession of a permanent green card. That's the way the scheme was supposed to unravel.

But to kill time, the newlyweds began dating. Then they completely fouled up the arrangement by procreating. Twice.

The two-year limit came and went, and they settled into life as a real family.

But after 16 years, Ike's arranged wife grew tired of his drinking—a vice that consisted entirely of a heroic intake of Corona Beer—and she booted him out of the Chicago home they had purchased with proceeds from fake Coach purses imported from the Philippines and sold in the black markets of Los Angeles.

The deterioration of his marriage wasn't without warning. His extreme beer habit had cost him his 25-year job as a hospital administrator, an ideal front for their illegal import business, which in turn was showing flagging profits from neglect, which meant selling off some of the Chicago apartment buildings that their ill-gotten largesse had purchased.

One night during his decampment from his home (while drinking Corona, no doubt), Ike heard Bob Seger's "Hollywood Nights," and—apparently missing the point of the cautionary tale—he zeroed in on the

A GOOD LOOK BEFORE DARK

fateful decision of the song's anti-hero, who "headed West 'cause he felt that a change would do him good; see some old friends, good for the soul."

Ike's first phone call to me indicated that he'd just be passing through the Bay Area. His second tested the waters for a slightly more extended stay.

A month later, after he'd been polluting my living room with empty Corona bottles for more than a week, he finally came clean: California was his destiny. Eureka!

Ike had a heart of gold and some money in the bank. On the other side of the ledger, he had no car, little chance of recovering his driver's license (even in a new state), no job prospects ... and little ambition. He was hopelessly mired in the past, specifically 1980-84, when he partied his way through DePaul University.

When I told him that I had no interest in re-creating the dormitory years, Ike looked at me like I'd just demythologized Santa Claus. In my struggle to come up with some consolatory words, I actually said: "But hey, you're welcome to stay in California."

"Thanks," Ike replied. "I mean, thank you, Governor Higgins, sir."

The next day, I introduced him to my landlord, who I knew would look past his employment situation upon my recommendation. A few days later, he was living in an apartment overlooking the pool, the perfect location for a man of leisure unencumbered by a career, family or, for that matter, a stick of furniture.

Despite no formal schedule, Ike was a stickler for routine. He rose at 5:30 each morning. Thirty minutes later, he was the first customer to grace the doorway at

Dave's Liquor Store, a half-mile away. He harvested a 12-pack. By noon, one dozen glass soldiers had been memorialized in the recycling bin. Ike, not quite as sure of foot as he was in his first excursion of the day, then returned to Dave's to secure his provisions for the afternoon: another 12-pack. Rarely did food make the cut. The day I cleaned out his scant belongings, 14 months after he signed his lease, his refrigerator and oven were as pristine as the day he moved in. And not because he was picky about cleanliness.

That routine caught up with him on May Day, 2002. As I was decompressing from my meeting about my doomed future in the journalism business, Ike walked across the footbridge separating our apartment buildings and knocked on my door, asking me to call 911 because he was bleeding from his anus.

* * *

May 2:
Midnight – 8 A.M.

At one minute after midnight on May 2, I burst through the doors of an emergency room.

Someone with a credential hanging from his neck soon directed to me to a room, said a few words about the virtues of patience, closed the door behind him and left me to my own devices with a depressing array of literary choices. I picked up a copy of "Diabetic Living."

This was death's doorstep, the intensive care unit at Highland Hospital in Oakland, where the indigent, stacked up like cordwood in the hallways, received a final indignity from Planet Earth.

When I couldn't read another word, I glanced back

at the clock. It was nearly 1 a.m., and the walls of the tiny waiting room were closing in around me. I was now officially pissed. The not-so-helpful visiting room employee who had deposited me here had disappeared in the labyrinth of hallways in this Steven King-inspired ward for the soon-to-be-interred, never to be seen again. I was on my own. Exasperated, I pushed through the door of my holding pen, determined to find my friend.

I wasn't prepared for all the triaged souls strapped to gurneys on both sides of the hallway, turn after turn. I decided, there and then, that I would never again be without medical coverage, no matter how thin my budget. It was surreal from my angle. I can't imagine how terrifying it must have been through the eyes of the doomed.

I finally located Ike among the masses, seizing from detoxification, but thankfully heavily sedated. His nurse asked me how I'd gained entry. "Not with anyone's help around here," I replied.

"What happened to him?" I asked.

"He was bleeding out when we got him and he went right into surgery," she said, summarizing three hours on an operating table. "Who are you?"

I pulled out my business card, which identified me as a sportswriter for the *Oakland Tribune*. The nurse started to hand it back to me like the worthless credential it was in this setting. "He doesn't have any relatives in California," I explained, pointing to my cell number. "Please hold on to this as his contact number."

Although I had seen him just a few hours earlier, it was hard to believe that the haggard, shaking wreck of a human on the gurney was my buddy from college.

I should have known something was amiss on the final day of April, the day before his fateful knock on my door, when Ike stopped by and took me up on my offer to share the Chinese food I had just pulled from the microwave. He rarely accepted my offers of food; he didn't like to pollute his buzz with nutrition. But he had no beer that day, nor the day before, he said, because he was feeling off his game. Ike had foreseen that scenario, as well. His standard response to my pleas for moderation during his year-plus stay in California was one that he always delivered with deadly conviction: "If I stop drinking," he insisted, "I'll die."

In the early hours of May 2, however, the ICU nurse did a pretty good job of convincing me that he was out of the woods.

"That won't be necessary," she said when I asked her if I should call Chicago to put his two kids, both young teenagers, on a plane to say good-bye to their father. "Things could have gone a lot worse in surgery. But he's stabilized now and he'll be under heavy sedation while he's detoxing."

"How long will that be?" I asked.

"Maybe four of five days," she replied. I was holding my hardcover copy of Jimmy Buffett's *A Pirate Looks at Fifty*, 450 pages of pure escapism. The title was borrowed from Buffet's own song, *A Pirate Looks at Forty*, a tune that Ike had played over and over on his recent 40th birthday. My friend needed some escapism now. But upon hearing that he wouldn't be reading anything for the better part of the next week, I tucked the book into my backpack.

His seemingly stable condition assuaged some of the guilt I felt for losing track of my friend in the hours leading up to my frantic search through Highland Hospital. Ike was not above bellyaching about this malady or that—I sometimes referred to him as my 80-year-old college classmate—and I had heard the boy cry 'wolf' a few too many times to be phased by his request to call 911.

"You can't retract a 911 call," I said, throwing Ike the phone and calling his bluff. "But you do what you gotta do." He didn't hesitate in pushing the buttons.

In the 10 minutes or so that passed between his call and the arrival of the EMTs, Ike returned to being his usual jovial self. He even joked with the EMT crew as they strapped him in the gurney. One of them told me that passing blood was indeed a serious matter. Unconvinced, I told Ike to give me a call when they had given him a clean bill of health at the hospital on the island where we lived. I waved good-bye and told him I'd see him in a few hours. I went back upstairs, finished working on a feature story for the Sunday paper and went to the gym for a workout.

I didn't start to worry until I returned home. My voicemail was empty. I called the local hospital in Alameda, but they had no record of him. I called the nearest hospital in Oakland, but had no luck there, either. I was starting to feel panicky. Finally, one of my calls led me to a nurse who, upon learning that Ike lacked insurance, directed me to Highland, the county's dumping ground for such cases. I tracked him down in the ICU, no thanks to anyone working there.

When I mentioned that I was Ike's only local contact, the ICU nurse inquired about his wedding band. I was taken aback, because a few months earlier I had convinced Ike to remove his ring in order to acknowledge his divorce and move on. Upon closer inspection, his wedding band had been replaced with something far cheaper.

"Oh, that doesn't mean anything," I said, oblivious

to the legal entanglement I was weaving. "That's from his wedding in the Philippines a few weeks ago."

That much was true. Although his Filipina wife left him, Ike never got the Philippines out of his system. Even after their dubious import business went the way of their marriage, Ike spent months at a time in the islands, where the money that was quickly drying up in California went a lot further. And it bought things, like affection, that weren't open-market commodities in the states.

I do not begrudge Ike the comfort he found among the women of that service-oriented culture. He had a kind word for everybody, and drinking only brought out his gregariousness. He was the quintessential friendly drunk. He would occasionally call me with updates of his travels. He was always pleasantly intoxicated, with beer and beauty. He was as happy as anyone could be who was nursing a broken heart and desperately missing his children. And who doesn't wish such illusions for their friends?

But then he went and married one of his comforters. For all his worldliness, Ike very often displayed childlike naiveté.

To wit: On an earlier trip to the islands, he informed me that he would be letting a friend use his apartment while he was overseas. When pressed, Ike admitted the friend was really an acquaintance from the corner bar (the one that shared wall space with Dave's Liquor Store), a reprobate named Rocky who sometimes slept behind the dumpster at McDonald's. I knew the guy by reputation—he was a local meth addict who found himself homeless when his mother was evicted from our complex, allegedly for her son's illicit activities. I advised Ike that he was making a big mistake, but he had already turned over the keys. After all, he told me, it wasn't as though he had anything worth stealing.

I forgot about the arrangement until a week later, when I received a distressed, early-morning call from our landlord. Upon rolling into the office, she discovered a litany of voicemails from neighbors complaining of loud and prolonged partying at Ike's apartment – strange, since she knew Ike was in the Philippines. Upon entering the apartment, she was shocked to find dozens of beer bottle caps inserted into the popcorn stucco ceiling, the unmistakable haze of methamphetamine hanging heavy in the air, and the pipes used to ingest it scattered willy-nilly around the apartment. In the midst of the carnage was Rocky, laid out as if he'd walked into a right cross by Apollo Creed.

Once roused into consciousness, Rocky informed the landlord that he had Ike's permission to use the place, and dropped my name as his reference. When I arrived at the scene, I cursed Ike from afar ... then lied and told the landlord I'd never heard Rocky's name, let alone been contacted by Ike about the arrangement.

Enraged, Rocky began to gather his instruments of self-destruction. He was obviously practiced at being evicted and thus traveled lightly. Unbeknownst to me, a financial windfall was about to present itself. Our landlord, a paunchy, middle-aged woman who was fond of me as a tenant, discovered one of the pipes that Rocky had overlooked in his haste to clear out. Not wanting any further trouble, she extended her hand to offer him his paraphernalia. Snatching the pipe in a violent gesture, he addressed her by the one word that I find intolerable under any circumstances.

"Give me that, you cunt," he raged, snatching it out of her hands.

I hadn't laid my hands on another man in anger 13

years, since defending myself against Roshni at McDonough's Pub in Savannah on that night of insanity in Savannah in 1989. I'd been familiar with the term "fighting words" since I was a kid on the tarred playgrounds of St. Thomas the Apostle.

In a journalism law class at Southern Illinois, however, I learned that the term had a legal definition. In 1942, the U.S. Supreme Court established the "Fighting Words Doctrine" by a 9-0 decision in Chaplinsky vs. New Hampshire. The court held that "insulting or fighting words, those that by their very utterance inflict injury or tend to incite an immediate breach of peace" were among the "well-defined and narrowly limited classes of speech" not protected by the First Amendment.

As a journalist who held the First Amendment sacred, I deemed myself to be the ideal arbiter for this particular situation. I came to the quick conclusion that Rocky had strayed outside of his constitutional rights to not have me punch him in the face. So that's what I did.

"You asshole," I said, enjoying some free speech of my own as I dropped him to his previous position— prone, next to the empty pizza box—with a perfect shot to the jaw. "You don't *ever* talk to her like that."

My landlord didn't raise my rent for years.

I wanted to strangle Ike for the drama he had facilitated, but he's not the kind of guy to whom grudges stick. He apologized upon returning home, and that was that.

Stateside, he relished his deck overlooking the pool. Not because he had much use for pools, but because the location provided him a forum to interact with our fellow residents. Everybody liked Ike. On many days, his only non-liquid caloric intake came from a sausage or hamburger offered by one of the neighbors using the common grills beside the pool. It was there that I spotted Ike after a run one day after his return from the Philippines. He was flush with something akin to love. He informed me that he had married one of the young women who had been part of his travel narratives for the better part of year.

In his Utopian world, he had grand plans to usher his new bride through the complex stages of immigration. He figured he'd have her by his side in California in four years, five tops.

In the meantime, Ike had a more pressing issue: the rent that was coming due in May would empty his bank account.

He solved that problem in nearly identical fashion as Ben Sanderson, the character portrayed by Nicolas Cage in *Leaving Las Vegas*: Ike simply timed his life to end when the money ran out.

I received the news via voicemail early on May 2, several hours after I left the hospital, having been assured by his ICU caretaker that Ike was out of the woods. I was on the phone with another college buddy, relaying the news that our friend might really be in trouble this time, and let the incoming call pass when I didn't recognize the number on my caller ID.

The message came in broken English, a doctor whose job that morning—maybe every morning—was to play the role of Grim Reaper. The message was ruthlessly efficient: "Mr. Higgins, this is Dr. So-and-So. I would like to inform you that Ike died at 7:59 this morning. Please call me with any questions."

* * *

8 A.M. – 4 P.M.

I skipped right past the "denial" stage of the Kübler-Ross grieving model and went straight for anger. I wasted more than an hour vainly trying to track down the ghoulish M.D. who would leave such a message for anyone—including Ike's kids, as far as the doctor knew—to discover on voicemail. But Dr. Death's tracks were well covered. As far as Highland Hospital was concerned, he was a ghost.

I had no idea what to do next. Ike had a dysfunctional relationship with his family. I had never met his parents or siblings.

I was fairly well-acquainted with his ex-wife, with whom I had been friendly during headier years of their relationship. But I was harboring resentment toward her now because of the way she had abandoned the same miscreant she married. I had no intention of calling her. I knew next to nothing about his siblings, only that one brother had died an addict's death several years earlier and another taught at the University of Chicago. Of his parents, I knew only that they were Polish emigrants, and that his father had died a year earlier, on Mother's Day. And now I was charged with calling the survivors and delivering another Mother's Day surprise.

Fortunately Ike's family surname was so ethnically Polish, filled with consonants. Even in his hometown of Chicago, a city whose Polish population was surpassed only by Warsaw, there were only a few listings. There were two listings with the first name of "John." One of the few things I did know about his family was that his late father and his living brother were named John. I called the first number and found my intended recipient.

A GOOD LOOK BEFORE DARK

Adding considerable weight to the usual awkwardness of a death call to the family – the first one I'd ever had to make – was the fact that I first had to introduce myself and explain my relationship to Ike.

Near the end of the call, I asked the professor to extend my sincere sympathies to his mother. Professor John informed me that he'd rather not have that conversation. He gave me her phone number and asked me to make that call, as well.

I mildly protested on the grounds that a call from her only surviving son would be more appropriate than one from a total stranger, given the situation. He replied as he might to a dull freshman enrolled in one of his classes.

"On the contrary, Brian. It would be entirely appropriate for you to update our mother on the situation."

The *situation*? Christ. Ike hadn't exaggerated about his familial dysfunction.

His mother responded exactly as her son had. No wailing and gnashing of teeth. Just a long, resigned sigh, as if she had been waiting for this news for years.

In turn, she asked me to be inform Ike's ex-wife and the mother of her grandchildren. I protested with a bit more vehemence. Suddenly, Ike's mom could only speak Polish.

I dialed the number for my third conversation of the morning, cursing the name of Alexander Graham Bell. The ex made it unanimous by receiving the news with detached inevitability, as if I had told her that her car had been towed from in front of a fire hydrant.

It may have been some passive-aggression that made me inquire about her new husband, a union about which Ike was informed by his children a few months earlier. That bit of news had, in my mind, been the catalyst for his acceleration into the abyss.

She hesitated before beginning her confession: She hadn't married anyone. She had merely been attempting to convince her ex-husband, in his consistently altered state, that a reunion wasn't in the cards. My head began to spin. As much as I understood the motive, I couldn't imagine any scenario in which she thought it acceptable to make their children complicit in the scheme.

I told none of them about Ike's new bride half a world away. I thought it best that he take that secret to his grave.

But I had inadvertently denied him that option when I opened my mouth to the graveyard-shift nurse in the ICU 10 hours earlier. Four days later, when the professor called the Alameda County coroner's office to inquire why his brother's body had not arrived on an arranged flight, he was informed that Ike's next of kin in the Philippines had refused to sign the papers releasing his body ... until she had been provided a copy of his will.

As I hung up the phone with his ex-wife, I was overcome with exhaustion. This was shaping up to be epic day. It was not yet noon. I went back to bed.

$$* * *$$

4 P.M. – Midnight

The softball team on which I served as player-coach was scheduled for the early-evening game on May 2. Having slept just a few hours, I gave up, showered and

A GOOD LOOK BEFORE DARK

drove to the field. I needed an escape. I had considered blowing off the game and heading to Mount Diablo for a grueling hike—physical exertion was my drug of choice when I was overwhelmed by circumstance—but ultimately decided that letting the inmates run the asylum wasn't the best course of action for my cellar-dwelling softball team.

Within months of my 40th birthday, I was at the tail end of a downward athletic spiral that had taken me from shortstop to left field to second base to right field to third base to first base. Playing first base required as much physical exertion as flipping the channels on a TV, but it did require focus (especially given the wild proclivities of my infielders). Seeing as how I was desperate to focus on something other than Ike's body on a coroner's slab, I showed up early, ran a couple of hard laps to quiet the demons and was stretching when Mike, my closest friend on the team, showed up with his new girlfriend.

Mike and I had known each other for less than two years, but we had bonded strongly over two pursuits— softball and hiking. Mike introduced me to a side of California, the part above sea level, that would come to play such a vital role in my life. Under his guidance, I fell in love with the trails of Mount Diablo and Mount Tamalpais. He introduced me to the grandeur of Yosemite, as well. We came to relish what we referred to as our "mountain time."

I didn't know it, but those times were soon to end. Mike had moved to the west coast to accept a lucrative executive position and put some distance between him and his native Atlanta, where the pain of a recent divorce was a bit too palpable. He was in the process of falling in love with his new girlfriend, and they would soon return to his hometown, buy a house together and, as far as I know, live happily ever after. But he left me with the ultimate parting gift: a love for hiking that would put me on a path toward a woman that would change my life.

But that evening, I was grateful for the California sunshine and the life-affirming noises of competition reverberating across the field as both dugouts filled with players.

My team sucked, and we were already trailing when I came to bat for the first time in the bottom of the second inning. I was known throughout the league as a dead pull-hitter, meaning that I lacked the talent to do anything with the bat except swing hard to my strong side. Being a right-hander, that meant that everybody except the shortstop, third baseman and left fielder could go for a smoke when I came to the plate. I had played in the league for years, and virtually every player on every opposing team was aware of my limitations.

So I was hardly the only one in the park with a surprised look on my face when I hit a towering shot over the head of the center fielder.

I have loved the Cincinnati Reds since I was old enough to understand the game and I grew up idolizing Pete Rose—a.k.a. Charlie Hustle—a player of limited natural ability who made extraordinary things happen by never passing up an opportunity to be aggressive. It's a philosophy that he had a hard time leaving on the field (I can attest to the chaos such a demeanor invites in the real world), but I learned at an early age to appreciate base-running as an art form.

At 6-foot-2 and upwards of 250 pounds, nobody has ever accused me of being fast, but I had my mind set on a double the instant the ball left the bat. I did not stray from my conviction, even after the outfielder circled around and grabbed the ball on a single hop before I reached first base. As I chugged around the

A GOOD LOOK BEFORE DARK

bag and headed for second, he relayed a perfect strike to his cutoff man, who wheeled and fired a rifle shot toward my destination.

Covering the bag at second was the shortstop, the smallest player in the league. Chris Brickley weighed scarcely 150 pounds soaking wet. Despite his stature, Chris bordered on cocky. He played on a traveling baseball team on the weekends and considered softball a brand of weekday slumming. Until that day, our relationship consisted entirely of small talk on the field of play. Henceforth, we would become close friends, bound in blood (mine).

The throw had so much mustard on it that I could hear the stitching cutting a path through the air as I approached second with a hard slide, cleats in the air in an attempt to back Chris off the play.

Unfortunately for me, the tactic worked. At the very last moment, Chris decided it wasn't worth the cost. He hurtled my legs, abandoning the throw … which sailed like a cannonball into my left eye socket. My world went black.

I don't think I actually went unconscious at any point, because I distinctly remember a thought common to victims of trauma: "I can't believe this is happening to *me*." I also remember thinking: "I should be feeling more pain than I am."

As I rolled from my back onto my stomach, the bargaining began. Maybe the darkness is only temporary. Maybe being blind in just one eye wouldn't be so bad.

The opponent's third baseman later told me that the ball colliding with my skull "was the sickest sound I've ever heard." Both teams had instinctually rallied around me at second base. I could smell the thick fear emanating from the group. It struck me that if I could alleviate some of their trepidation, maybe they wouldn't be able to transfer so much of it back to me.

"I still haven't heard you call me safe, Bobby!" I said, invoking the name of the infield umpire. The laughter sliced through the tension and the resulting chatter made me feel better. Maybe there was a chance that there was no permanent damage. But I had little doubt that any chances of a modeling career had come to a screeching halt.

I became aware that my eyes were actually closed, a hopeful sign. I opened them slowly, but no light filtered through. I could feel the blood dripping from what seemed like every pore in my face, which actually spawned another surge of hope. Maybe the blood had pooled over my eyes and was blocking the light. I scraped away what felt like a gallon of goop from the front of my face. But the blackness prevailed. As I reached up to scrape off another layer, my hand collided with a pair of shinbones. More hope. Maybe I couldn't see because I was positioned at the bottom of a densely forested valley of legs.

I begged for some space. I could hear Mike commanding everybody to step back. I opened my eyes yet again. Coming into focus, some 75 feet away, was the scorekeeper, Larry, huddled in the press box behind the chain-link backstop. Larry wasn't a pretty man. But he was a beautiful sight to behold.

While teammates and opponents alike attempted to staunch the bleeding with the gauze and Ace bandages rummaged from a half-dozen bags, Mike pulled his truck onto the field. Somebody had called 911, but Mike figured he could be at the local hospital before the ambulance even arrived at the field.

A GOOD LOOK BEFORE DARK

Five minutes later, I could have sworn I heard the snort of a suppressed chuckle from the nurse manning the desk as Mike guided my bulbously wrapped head into the emergency room like a Macy's Thanksgiving float. "Is this the work of a medical professional?" she asked as she probed my head for a starting point to begin the de-twining.

"My, my," she continued, "I haven't seen this sort of technique since Sherman stormed Atlanta."

Now it was my turn to laugh. Mike, like any good Southerner, still harbored resentment about the burning of his hometown 138 years earlier. I paid the price. Laughing was excruciating.

As it happened, Alameda Hospital had won a stay of execution several weeks earlier, when voters in our island city had, by the slimmest of margins, approved an emergency funding proposition to keep the hospital open. I soon got a sense of why things might have been a bit shaky on the financial front. I could hear a baby in the treatment area, but I was the only patient in the waiting room. Nonetheless, three hours passed before I saw a doctor.

The infant, who was being treated for an ear infection, wailed like a siren for the duration. To all the parents of the all the babies who have ever felt compelled to tell me about their sleepless nights in the service of a crying newborn, I now feel compelled to respond: You have only roamed in the lower minor leagues of annoyance-by-child until every atom in your broken, Humpty Dumpty head has been split by 180 minutes of unabated howling from a baby with whom you have no genetic investment.

A nurse eventually untangled the yardage mummifying my skull, lecturing me all the while that the three pounds of infield dirt entombed in the gauze wasn't making her life any easier. As my teammates dropped by to gawk and unfavorably compare my visage to Mel Gibson's character in *Man Without A Face*, I received doubly-depressing news: They had lost another one for the Gipper; and Carl, who pinch-ran for me at second base after I was carted off, had somehow been thrown out at third despite the batter behind me cracking a clean hit to right field.

My blood had been spilled in vain.

Upon that last bit of news, the nurse took pity on me. She shooed away my teammates and injected me with the sweet nectar of morphine.

I considered myself a fairly well-season traveler through the valley of pleasure-inducing substances, but that was my first experience with anything injected. The baby's unrelenting wail wasn't the soundtrack I would have chosen for my first such trip. But in my newly enlightened state I decided that it was no worse than the Grateful Dead.

Mike was driving me home when the digital clock on his dashboard hit midnight. A zipper of several dozen stitches ran through my entire left eyebrow to the bridge of my nose, a facial Mason-Dixon line that would never fully heal.

"Man, they dealt this day off the bottom of the deck," I said to Mike, who nodded in agreement as a Counting Crows song spilled softly from his truck's radio.

But I had survived May 2, 2002. As my buzz receded, I began to come to terms with the fact that one of my dear friends had not.

12

Juror 5

When the 2002 football season ended, the shit hit the fan. The *Oakland Tribune* had hired a hatchet man named Howard. His job was to intimidate employees. Howard did this primarily by invading traditional spatial barriers and making employees feel ill at ease on the job. Howard's M.O. was to move his chair to within 18 inches of a copy editor and stare, silently, at his work for 30 or 40 minutes at a time. Well, it wasn't exactly in silence.

He was morbidly obese and his heavy breathing filled the air. The stench of Howard's unwashed crevices was repugnant. In the airless space of the small office where he liked to have foreboding one-on-one meetings when he wasn't creeping out employees in the newsroom, it was often difficult to suppress the urge to vomit.

Several other beat writers had joined me in filing a union complaint against the paper for capriciously assigning writers to the copy desk. When said shit hit said fan, however, they capitulated. I did not. I was as infuriated as I was repulsed by Norman's increasingly frequent one-on-one meetings with me. In the final one, he asked me if I was ready to stop being a petulant child and assume my off-season seat at the copy desk. I stood up, told him to wash his cheese-ripe ass, and walked out of the newsroom forever.

I was proud of myself. I had stood my ground on principal when all others had caved. Finally, something to remember fondly on my deathbed.

Besides, marketing paid much better. My personality was ideally suited for it and my media connections made me attractive to clients and employers.

The years rolled along. It had been a long while since my weekends were free. After Mike returned to Atlanta to marry his girlfriend, I took to solo-hiking, becoming intimately familiar with those very trails that I had glimpsed from the cockpit of Scott's training Cessna so many years before. In the marketing world, my schedule was suddenly aligned with the masses, with weekends off and all, and I began recruiting friends to hike with me. I liked seeing the looks in their eyes when we rounded a corner or crested a hill and were greeted by a breathtaking panorama below. And there was no lack of those.

I had a knack for organizing and leading. I had been doing it since I was a kid, arranging teams and schedules for our backyard whiffle ball leagues. After college, I started an annual Blizzard Bowl co-ed flag football tournament in my hometown, contested in the snow and chill of February. At the workplace, I was invariably the guy assigned to organize the annual out-of-office event. In my first year in California, I started a March Madness basketball pool. The first year, 12 guys kicked in $20 bucks apiece on a golf course. By the 20th

A GOOD LOOK BEFORE DARK

year, the pool was worth $30,000 and consisted of hundreds of people across the nation.

So I was geekily prepared when word of my weekend hikes spread and the crowds grew. I'd show up an hour early and trace our hike route on park maps for each of the attendees, even though most couldn't read trail maps and the rest could have cared less.

But I was caught off guard when I wound up leading another group altogether in 2009.

* * *

In all the fields of human endeavor, nothing begs for the uninvited opinion of friends and strangers quite like a jury summons.

"Tell 'em you hate black people," said Frank, a guy at my gym, when I read him the summons in the locker room.

"Would you do that?" I inquired.

"Hell, yes. In a heartbeat," he replied.

"But you're black."

"And you don't see my black ass sittin' in a jury box, do you?"

Because so many inhabitants of California live off the grid, those of us who are registered to vote receive jury notices like junk mail. In my first 15 years as a registered voter in various states, I received one jury summons. In my next 15 years—during which I lived in California—I received 12. Long about my seventh or eighth notice, my luck ran out.

"Tell them you're having sex with a cop," said Larisa, a frumpish cop who lived in my building.

What if they ask for details?" I said, thinking a judge or lawyer might call my bluff.

"Then tell them it's kinky sex," she said, winking.

In the end, I decided to play it straight on my 10-page Alameda County Superior Court questionnaire, which I filled out with 119 of my fellow potential jurors in the ground-floor room built for herding potential jurors. Blaring at us from a half a dozen TV screens was an endlessly looping video informing us that jury duty was our patriotic opportunity to make amends for not serving our country in World War II.

The questions, written by the lawyers in the case with the judge's approval, left no doubt that we were dealing with a criminal trial. I was relieved, for I had been dreading the possibility of being called to serve on a case involving a property-line dispute or some such civil nonsense.

My journalism career was behind me when I received the summons in April 2009, but a reporter's curiosity never dies. After completing the questionnaire, my half of the jury pool still had quite a bit of time to kill before being summoned upstairs for a briefing by the judge. I approached one of the deputies behind the counter.

"So what happens if you don't show up for jury duty?" I asked, figuring this might be my lone opportunity to hear an expert weigh in on the age-old water-cooler question.

"Depends on the judge," he said. "And then it depends on what side of the bed the judge got up on."

As he put it, superior court judges were generally too busy to be bothered with such matters. But some were known, when the mood struck them, to issue bench warrants for truant jurors.

A GOOD LOOK BEFORE DARK

"Hard to believe any cop would have time to carry out something like that," I said, "especially here in Oakland."

"That's true," the deputy replied. "But a bench warrant is like a nice little surprise waiting for you at the bottom of the Cracker Jack box the next time you get pulled over for rolling through a stop sign."

At long last, we were ushered to the seventh floor. That's when the real theater began.

My eyes were instantly drawn to the statuesque assistant district attorney who would be handling the case, a beautiful African-American woman with a porn-star name: Danielle Hilton. I was sitting near the back, and it was pretty obvious that Ms. Hilton was being visually assaulted by a solid majority of the jury pool, men and women.

But the incontrovertible star of the courtroom was the Honorable Thomas J. Reardon.

He introduced us to Ms. Hilton, then to the public defender, Barbara Dickinson, an engaging, energetic package in a small bundle. A vastly experienced barrister, this was to be her final case as a criminal defense attorney. As she would tell me in so many words after the trial, she had reached the limit of her endurance on that particular rotation in the public defender's office. By the end of the trial, I would understand in full.

Finally came the defendant, straight out of central casting: a black man from the frontier streets of East Oakland, hair tightly wired to his skull in cornrows. A lazy eye made him appear both sympathetic and unhinged.

It turned out that I needn't have worried about an insidious civil case. The defendant was charged with raping two young girls, both of whom were autistic. Any lingering folly among the potential jurists vanished upon that pronouncement. The room got very quiet.

Although it's hardly ever a part of *Law & Order* or other courtroom dramas, voir dire—the process of selecting the jury—is one of the most intriguing parts of the American judicial process. At least it was for me. For only in voir dire do you get to hear all those excuses that ill-informed friends and colleagues give you for avoiding jury duty trotted out in front of a real judge.

And Judge Thomas Reardon was a master of the game.

First up was a pretty young blonde who had apparently honed a quick dismissal strategy based on "a general distrust of black people." Her philosophy degree from an Eastern liberal arts college hadn't prepared her for the interrogation that followed. At one point, the judge pointed out an African-American gentleman sitting near me in the back of the room and asked Little Miss Homecoming Queen why he wasn't worthy of her trust. She didn't know him, she admitted, so she really couldn't say. "Well then," the judge continued, "do you know the defendant?"

"No, but ..."

"Speak up. This is America. You have a right to be heard."

"No, but ... but the police arrested him, right?" she said, stammering where she had been cocksure minutes earlier.

"Yes, according to the record, the defendant was arrested. That's generally how they wind up at trial."

"Well, they usually don't arrest innocent people,"

she countered.

"Is that so?" replied the judge. "What if I told you that he was arrested by a black police officer?"

"Oh," she said.

"I'm not saying that he was," the judge continued, "but it's certainly a possibility. Quite a conundrum, eh?"

Her face was as red as her lipstick. Even the people around her were squirming.

At that point, the judge released his death grip, as he would do with several more of my fellow would-be jurors just as they barreled into the intersection of Foot & Mouth. "Wow," I whispered in admiration to a square-jawed guy named Eric with whom I struck up a conversation in the hallway during one of the breaks. "This guy knows how to play an audience."

"Yeah," Eric agreed. "He definitely commands the room."

Turns out we weren't wrong. After the trial, I found a public radio interview with Judge Reardon online. The subject: his starring role in a local community theater production of *The Music Man.*

When voir dire continued, the judge asked us a question that may have been devised to demonstrate just how far we had drifted since high school civics classes. If we were forced to render a verdict based solely on what we knew of the defendant at that very moment, what say we?

The first three people to raise their hand seemed bound and determined to distance themselves from the foot-in-mouth blonde. They assured the judge that they were independent thinkers whose opinions wouldn't be formed until they heard the facts in the case. Judge

Reardon pressed his lips together, as if they were puppies who had peed on the carpet.

The fourth person upon whom he called, a man who had been raised in India, was brief and unequivocal.

"He's innocent," the man said.

"And why is that?" the judge inquired.

"Because in America you are presumed innocent until the prosecution meets the burden of guilt." He later told me that he had memorized his answer as part of his citizenship course.

"There you have it, folks," Judge Reardon said. "So the defendant, as he sits before you, is …?"

He turned back to the distressed blonde, who was so relieved to receive some guidance that she practically barked the answer: "Innocent!"

And with that, he let her off the hook. But neither he nor the attorneys dismissed her from duty for quite a while, a smoking piece of wreckage left at the scene for the next jurors contemplating an easy exit to assess.

Not that it stopped some from trying. One man, whose parents had emigrated from Asia, claimed to have such a distrust of police and the criminal justice system that he didn't even call the cops after being mugged in broad daylight in downtown Oakland. The judge pried back the lid a bit and got the guy to admit that, two days later, he was accosted by the same perpetrator at the same intersection. When asked by his mugger if he had called the cops, he informed him that he had not—and was promptly thanked and relieved of his wallet once again.

At that point, jaws throughout the jury pool slackened. Surely, somebody this daft would not be permitted to sit on a jury. Once again, however, neither the prosecution nor defense made an immediate move to dismiss him, continuing a chess game that befuddled a great many of us who lacked legal training.

And it wasn't merely the fools who were trotted out as cautionary tales. One smartly dressed woman took the opportunity to expound on her background as a Harvard law professor. It was proceedings like this, she espoused, which were the backbone of the criminal justice system in these United States. I found her to be interesting and well-spoken.

The legal eagles being paid to be in the courtroom, however, obviously saw her through different lenses. By the time she finished with her little soliloquy, the judge and opposing council had sharpened their claws to a shiny point. Their coordinated attack upon her Ivy League tower was something to behold. At the end, Miss Hilton tossed her exquisitely braided hair over her shoulder, thanked the law professor for her service and summarily dismissed her from jury duty. For a minute, I thought the judge, prosecutor and public defender were going to high-five one another.

After the trial, I was granted access to both trial attorneys, thinking I might write about the experience. One of the first questions I asked concerned the tire tracks they left on the law professor.

"She would have been poison in the jury room, giving everyone points of order," one told me. Said the other: "The stuff she teaches at Harvard has very little to do with the way it works down here in the trenches."

After watching them feed on her carcass, I felt sorry for the next juror they called to the stand.

"Brian Higgins," Judge Reardon announced,

shuffling to the next questionnaire on his desk.

"Christ on a cracker," I mumbled to Eric as I took my place in the open seat in the second row of the box.

"Mr. Higgins," Judge Reardon said, clearing his throat as I assumed the hot seat, "if there's one thing that judges and lawyers distrust more than law professors, it's probably members of the media."

"Former member of the media, your honor," I said, apologetically. "And I don't blame you."

Miss Hilton asked me if I would be tempted to write about the experience, a question which placed into my head the notion that the mystery defendant might be newsworthy. That, in turn, made me think that I might be walking into a trap to test what would be likely to violate the cardinal rule of the court, which was to avoid gathering any information about the defendant or any of the other players in this courtroom drama. Google was *verboten*.

I sputtered out the first thing that came to mind, which was something to the effect that my boss in my media relations position had other priorities for my time.

Miss Dickinson seemed satisfied with some basic information, in particular the fact that I was childless. The judge did a bit of probing around the section of my questionnaire in which I had displayed a little attitude about cops, based on some run-ins from my roguish past. But he seemed to sense that my anti-authoritarian streak had mellowed with age.

Indeed, I had come to appreciate Oakland's thin blue line, as corrupt as it sometimes was. Although I lived on an island, all five access points—four bridges and a tunnel—led to Oakland, where the murder rate was often among the nation's highest. Two years

A GOOD LOOK BEFORE DARK

earlier, just a few blocks from the courthouse in which I sat, a former colleague at the *Oakland Tribune* had been executed in broad daylight to silence his investigation of corruption and criminal activity at a local bakery that was serving as a front for a gang. In death, Chauncey Bailey became a national cause célèbre in the journalism world. Reporters from around the globe descended on Oakland to complete his work. Two years after my jury duty, Judge Reardon would preside over the trial and conviction of the man who had ordered Bailey's death.

Voir dire came to an abrupt ending soon after my interrogation. Most of us seated in the jury box were surprised by the screeching halt in the proceedings, since two dozen or so members of the jury pool had yet to have their day in court. As the preponderance of them gleefully fled the courtroom, one man spoke up.

"Excuse me," he said, standing to address the judge. "I've been sitting here for two days and you didn't even talk to me."

Judge Reardon handled him, too.

"What's your name, sir?"

"Roger."

"Well, Roger. What would you like to talk about?"

Roger seemed flustered.

"No, I mean … I just …"

"That was just a joke, Roger. Never let it be said that justice doesn't have a sense of humor."

Roger offered his last name and the judge quickly found his folder among the pile of jurors who hadn't been called to the stand.

"I won't take the liberty to speak for either

attorney, but I have no doubt that your name was discussed at some point over the last few days when the prosecutor and public defender were burning the midnight oil," the judge told Roger. "As one of my law professors once told me, sometimes that's just the way the jury crumbles."

* * *

We, the jury, ranged in age from a 27-year-old Hispanic woman—the only non-mother among the five females on the jury—to a 54-year-old white man, who, conversely, was the only male jurist with children. Two among us were immigrants, from Asia and Africa. During voir dire, the woman from Africa had not hidden her squeamishness for the subject matter of the trial, yet had made it by the public defender. Eric, my square-jawed hallway conversation partner—a veteran of Army special forces, as it turned out—didn't bat an eyelash during questioning. He, too, was on the jury.

We were assigned numbers by where we were sitting when the musical chairs of voir dire ended. I would be known in the record as Juror 5.

From start to finish, we were together for just over two weeks. But it was certainly a profound experience, for sitting on a criminal jury, especially one where the charges were so salacious, offered a unique view of the foundation upon which all of our constitutional rights are stacked. There are certainly cracks in the system. But I came away with the distinct feeling that, should I ever find myself in the dark place of defending myself against criminal charges, I'd happily take my chances with the American justice system. Then again, I'm a middle-class white guy.

A GOOD LOOK BEFORE DARK

I was easily the most extroverted member of the jury. I tried to relate, on some level, with all of my fellow jurors. I was certainly the only one among us who knew each of the other's names.

It was easier getting to know the men, simply because they were more willing to explore the sketchy area around the courthouse during our lunch break. The women generally packed their lunches and opted to read in the jury room, with the exception of the youngest member of the jury, who was attached to her cell phone when she wasn't in the jury box.

The Alameda County Courthouse is an architectural gem brimming with history, It was built in the early 1930s under the direction of Alameda County District Attorney Earl Warren, who would become governor of California and then Chief Justice of the U.S. Supreme Court. The front of the courthouse faces Lake Merritt, which in 1870 officially was designated as the first wildlife sanctuary in the U.S.

Diagonally across Lake Merritt is the Grand Lake district of Oakland, a trendy area filled with cafes and restaurants. But Grand Lake is a 3-mile round-trip walk from the courthouse, which didn't leave much time for lunch. Much closer was Chinatown, a poor cousin of the San Francisco version. In between the courthouse and Chinatown were the blighted outskirts of downtown Oakland. So the men on the jury traveled in packs and bonded over some really bad lunches and speculation about what Danielle Hilton did in her down time.

We needed the fraternal moments. The details of the case against the defendant were depressingly sordid. Day after day, the alleged depravity reached new depths. The prosecution strived to paint a picture of a defendant with a history of befriending women with autistic or mentally unstable daughters (or female foster children) who were easy prey for sexual exploitation. The defense did a solid job of pointing out the inconsistencies in Ms. Hilton's case.

It wasn't just the subject matter which was grinding. Judge Reardon pushed the pace. Several days before the case went to the jury, we had heard testimony from seven witnesses. After the trial, both Ms. Hilton and Ms. Dickinson told me that it was the first time in their respective careers that a judge had forced them to prepare for seven witnesses in a single day.

* * *

Instead of lunch on the day that the defense rested, Eric and I went for a run around Lake Merritt. He was in outstanding shape and a dozen years younger than me, and my legs were dragging from a brisk hike I had taken the prior evening at Redwood Regional Park. It was there that I often raced the fading, dappled sunlight up a lung-burning ravine. The park, which surrounds an observatory at the top of the Oakland hills, was my venue of choice when I only had an hour or two to drain the mental cesspool, and this trial had certainly filled my head with life's excrement.

Eric had already stretched and cooled down by the time I caught up with him on the trail below the courthouse. "We're going to be late" he said, militarily, striking fear in both our hearts that we might face the wrath of Judge Reardon.

Sure enough, the rest of the jury was awaiting our return. The buzzer from the courtroom sounded just as Eric and I rushed through the door into the jury room, signaling that the judge and lawyers were ready for our return. We also had a buzzer to signal that we were gathered and prepared.

"I can buy a minute or two," one of our fellow jurors seated next to the buzzer said. Eric and I rushed into the tiny bathroom to change out of our jogging gear. I toweled myself off, changed and applied deodorant, but I was still a sweaty mess when we filed into the courtroom to receive our instructions for deliberation.

Judge Reardon had a particular talent for explaining legal twists and turns in lay-friendly language, which is why his instruction for what came next seemed incomplete, as though he had abandoned a 2,000-piece jigsaw puzzle with just a few pieces remaining. The job of picking a jury foreperson would be left to our own devices. Apparently, we could arm-wrestle for the honor, if we so chose.

I wasn't really worried. Our jury, I thought, was filled with bright, reflective people, any number of whom would have made a good foreperson. I would have been opposed to only two: the youngest among us, who had avoided human contact outside the jury box in deference to her cell phone; and the woman seated directly to my right in the jury box—Juror No. 4—who emphatically nodded in agreement with practically every witness, plaintiff and defense, who swore an oath to tell the truth, the whole truth and nothing but the truth.

We were soon back on the eighth floor, which was reserved solely for jurors and the sheriff's deputies who guarded them. Our cramped jury room was predominantly occupied by a table for 12 and a whiteboard. It was so confining that only about half of our belongings—coats, purses, lunch coolers and the like—fit up against the wall. The rest of our stuff had to be piled on the lone window sill in the room. That window, which opened outward overlooking a busy crosswalk between the courthouse and another county building, was a godsend. Otherwise, our room would have been as claustrophobic as the defendants' holding cells lining the lower floors. The jury room abutted a tiny bathroom, through the walls of which every drop, plop and groan could be deciphered.

An hour after our run, my perspiration was somehow increasing in intensity. The first thing I did as everyone staked out a seat for the deliberation process was excuse myself to stick my head under the faucet and apply more deodorant. Deep breathing in that bathroom was normally an exercise conducted at one's own risk, but it had been empty for an hour, so I took the opportunity to do some yoga breathing to prepare for the weighty task ahead.

With mind and body renewed, I opened the door and stepped back into the jury room. The conversation immediately ceased. All eyes met mine.

I could feel my face flushing with embarrassment. I had a red-hot flash of déjà vu. I was transported back to Bexley Junior High. As I plodded up the back staircase following our 45-minute recess period during an icy Ohio January, a giggly conversation halted in mid-sentence. A half-dozen girls, some of them with mouths open in apparent disbelief, went silent as I approached. All of them had their gazes firmly locked on me as I trotted up the stairs, half-frozen and egregiously late for class.

Ten minutes earlier, Jimmy Messer, who at Age 15 had not yet progressed past the seventh grade and was rattlesnake-mean to boot, had horse-collared me in a game of "Smear the Queer" and hurtled me like a puck

A GOOD LOOK BEFORE DARK

across 25 feet of jagged ice. The violent game pitted the entire field against the guy stupid enough to be in possession of the ball, and the winter version of Smear The Queer was downright sadistic for guys like Jimmy Messer, who sent me skidding along the entire width of the basketball court that was buried beneath two feet of snow. I came to rest only when my thigh became lodged under the chain-link fence surrounding the court.

The harder I tried to extricate myself, the deeper the barbed end of the chain-link dug into my thigh and the decisively more sensitive adjacent area. Jimmy received an ovation for the takedown—even I had to admit the artistry in his game—and even took pity on me by checking on me as the other participants deserted the playground. But after attempting to rip me free of the fence through the use of brute force a couple of times, he abandoned the cause. "Sorry, dude. I already have three detentions this month," he said as he raced to beat the second bell.

It took me several minutes of squirming and kicking, but alas my blue jeans became disconnected from the fence. The temperature was in the single digits and I could no longer feel my extremities. Worse still, I'd probably be joining Jimmy in detention for being late. As I slipped in the back door of the school, I stomped my feet with all the grace of an elephant with a neurological disorder, desperately trying to regain some feeling in my feet before tackling the stairway to the classroom level.

The ruckus drew the attention of the fifth-period monitors, two girls in my seventh-grade class with superlative grades who patrolled the halls for stragglers and ne'er-do-wells. One of them was Susan, a tomboy with whom I was friendly. The other was Trish, one of the most coveted girls in the entire junior high. She had never given me the time of day, but now seemed to be giving me her full attention.

By the time I hit the landing and made a 180-degree turn toward the top of the stairwell, a half-dozen more girls had gathered around the railing, recruited out of the adjacent home economics class by Susan and Trish, no doubt.

As I moved out of the shadow of the landing onto the final half-dozen steps, all conversation died in its tracks. The eyes of every girl grew wide, and several covered their mouths to trap whatever venomous uttering was trying to escape. Never one to attract a harem, I grew more paranoid with every step. That's when I saw my blood-soaked sleeve. I was relieved; girls always made a bigger deal out of blood than was warranted. As I approached the top step, the girls parted, still silent, their eyes glued to what I thought was my bloody arm.

Trish broke the silence.

"Hiiiiii, Briiii-an," she said. "Looking good!"

"Oh that," I said, glancing downward in the direction of my hand, where I was beginning to feel trickles of blood pooling. "That's no big deal."

With that, the entire gaggle exploded in laughter and scattered, leaving me to ponder what had just transpired. Girls.

As I entered the bathroom to clean my arm, I caught site of myself in the full-length mirror. I stood there, frozen not by my struggle in near-zero temperatures, but by mortification.

The entire zipper area on my jeans was missing, and the underwear beneath was shredded like a battle flag. Poking out was my ice-blue, flash-frozen, prepubescent penis. Trish had a mole on her neck that was bigger.

"Brian!" Eric snapped, transporting me back to 2009 and the jury room, with 12 pairs of eyes transfixed on me. Dear God. If my penis was making another jailbreak, I'd soon enough have my own jury to contend with.

"Do you have anything to add?" Eric said, obviously agitated by my inattention.

"Sorry," I said. "I took a quick trip to Space Mountain. I'll go with whatever the rest of the group decides."

"That's great," Eric said. "Because we were just saying that you should be the foreman."

"Me?"

"Yeah, you're the only one who bothered to learn everyone else's name," said Colleen, a married woman with daughters. "And the judge didn't hate you."

Before I could respond that those were faint criteria for placing a man's fate in my hands, Eric jumped back in. "Any objections?"

There was none, so everyone obliged with a polite round of applause. With that, Colleen took some colored markers from the whiteboard, placed them in my hand and said, "No need to sit down. Lead the way, oh wise leader."

As I walked to the whiteboard trying to figure out what I should write on it, a new voice arose.

"Let's hope the rest of this process goes as quickly," said the girl with the cell phone.

* * *

In the interest of protecting a defendant's rights, we, the juries, rarely are permitted to see the big picture in any given trial … and are sometimes granted access to mere pixels. Judges and lawyers are constantly brokering deals about which truths will be dispensed to the jury, and which will not.

In the case of our trial, the wheeling and dealing in the judge's chambers reduced our scope so dramatically that it was as if we were watching an IMAX film on a 13-inch black-and-white TV with rabbit ears.

During the trial, of course, we didn't know that we were operating with blinders. Before the judge dismissed us for deliberations, he informed us that the charges had been reduced from rape to a form of improper touching. We were thoroughly confused. Through California's Three-Strikes Law, Danielle Hilton had constructed a platform on which to stack far lesser charges that would still turn convictions on both counts into an actuarial life sentence.

After a few hours of discussion, we were unanimous about convicting on the first count. The DNA evidence was irrefutable. It was a Thursday, and because the judge had been giving us Fridays off to catch up at our workplaces, it might have been our last day together. Except there was one holdout on the second count.

Thus did I find myself in the awkward position, as the jury foreman, of telling my colleagues that we were going to have to come back Monday morning because we had not yet deliberated long enough to be hung by a single juror—who just happened to be me. If looks could kill, I would have been disemboweled.

On the way home, I stopped at a video store and bought a copy of *12 Angry Men*. My plan was to study how Henry Fonda, the lone holdout in one of the most famous trials ever conceived for the silver screen, had turned 11 of his fellow jurors to his way of thinking. I had seen the movie as a kid, but watched it twice more that weekend. And I took notes.

On Monday morning, however, as I stared down 11 Frustrated Men and Women and reviewed my notes, Fonda's strategies betrayed me. After one impassioned plea for my fellow jurors to reconsider the motives they had assigned to the events of the day in question, the cell phone girl stopped rolling her eyes and spoke up for the first time without prompting. "Oh, I know that one!" she squealed with delight. "That's from *12 Angry Men*! My grandpa loves that movie!"

I hung my head and sat down as my fellow jurors descended on me like vultures feeding on carrion. I was hit with a hundred reasons why I was the one who needed to change his perspective. An hour later, my reasonable doubt had become unreasonable. Guilty on all charges.

As we were filing back to the jury room, Colleen sidled up next to me. "Are you going to look at the defendant when they read the verdict?" she asked. I had actually given that some thought over the previous days.

"Yes," I replied. "I think that's probably the right thing to do."

She shivered. "I'm not sure I could do it," she said, then gently patted my shoulder. "But I'm glad you are."

After identifying myself as the foreman, I breathed deeply, swallowed hard and leveled my gaze at the defendant as the verdict was read. I was grateful that he didn't look my way, not because it would have been threatening but because the moment likely would have lived on in perpetuity in the dark recesses of my skull if we had locked eyes. Then again, maybe he actually was staring at me with his wandering eye. If so, thank goodness for genetic defects.

In the weeks after the trial, my unreasonable doubt gnawed at me to the point that I committed an unreasonable amount of time to researching the matter. Both lawyers were generous with their time, and I called all the witnesses that had given me permission to do so after the verdict was read. I didn't know what I was going to do with the material. In fact, it became another unfinished project in a lifetime's library of unfinished projects. But in the process, I discovered the grisly truths to which we had not been entrusted as a jury. In summary, the defendant was guilty of far more than the sins for which we had convicted him.

I lost no more sleep contemplating if my doubt had been reasonable.

Colleen and I had agreed to meet for the sentencing two weeks later. We felt it would bring closure to our duty. The defendant, who was nearing 40 years of age, was sentenced to 55 years.

I walked her to her car and we said our good-byes, never to meet again. En route to my car, I reached into my backpack and began shuffling through the mail I had retrieved at my P.O. box. I discovered an official looking envelope from Alameda County. Inside was a check for my final week of jury duty, which amounted to just over $44.

I got to my car just as the meter maid disappeared around the corner. I pulled the ticket from my dashboard. It was a meter violation. I had outstayed the two-hour limit by mere minutes. I flipped the ticket around to check the fine for a meter violation. Scanning the final line, I spotted it: $45.

13

The Dark Side of the Moan

At an early age, I became frustrated with my inability to unlock the secrets of music. Guitar lessons didn't take. Piano lessons later in life were a waste of time. I had the innate ability to hold lyrics in my head for decades between actually hearing a particular song, but like so many of the talents I acquired at the Island of Misfit Toys gift shop, it held absolutely no monetary value on this or any nearby planet.

Lacking any discernable musical talent only fueled my passion for those who did. If I was never to be permitted access to the VIP Room of musicianship, I could at least give those on the other side of the velvet rope my full support. I became a live-music junkie. I sang in the shower. I was the first guy to pull a girl on the dance floor at a bar, wedding, funeral or concert. My youngest brother Dennis, a drummer who could pound out perfect percussion after listening to a song a few times, used to tell me that I had the rhythm of a bumble bee in a jar of peanut butter. But he also said that there was nobody with whom he'd rather attend a concert. I had the music in me, even if it sometimes took on a comical form when I expressed it to the world.

I snuck out of town to see my first concert, *Styx*, when I was 15. Two years later, after getting expelled from boarding school when a classmate ratted me out for taking a single hit off a joint, I passed out from smoking a heroic amount of weed at a concert in which 50,000 people cheered on *Cheap Trick*, *The Cars*, *Eddie Money* and *Todd Rundgren*. A year later, the week I graduated from high school, I lost the hearing in my right ear for a week after sitting next to the speaker at another *Todd Rundgren* concert (having been unconscious when he took the stage the year before).

And the good times have never stopped rolling, where my relationship with music is concerned. I've seen *The Who* from so close that I could count Roger Daltrey's chest hairs (none, he keeps it waxed) and *The Rolling Stones* from the very top row of the Gator Bowl, where a flirty girl who was pissed off at her date (for the shitty seats, no doubt) kept making passes at me. I've seen Eddie Vedder fall drunkenly on his ass and lay there laughing about it at *a Pearl Jam* concert, partied with the guys from my favorite band, *Toad The Wet Sprocket*, and told the siren-piped Margo Timmons, the lead singer for *Cowboy Junkies*, that her breathtaking "Angle Mine" would one day be my wedding song (hope you're not holding your breath, Margo).

My relationship with music has taken some warped twists. The first came my freshman year in college, when I was a DJ at WDPU, DePaul University's radio station. Today, WDPU is an award-winning, pioneering outlet among college radio stations. At the dawn of the 1980s, however, it was a broom closet transmitting by carrier-current expressly to other buildings at DePaul, primarily the cafeteria that sat two floors below the station in the Stuart Center. And because carrier-current stations weren't regulated by the FCC, the standards at WDPU were such that anyone who wanted a shift on the air invariably got one.

While Howard Stern was building a shock-jock empire on the East Coast, those of us in the Midwest were being transfixed by a rotund, bespectacled and unfiltered Chicago DJ named Steve Dahl, the man behind 1979's Disco Demolition Night, the event that thrashed half the outfield at the Chicago White Sox' Comiskey Park, forced a cancellation of the nightcap of their doubleheader with the Detroit Tigers and, most fortuitously, spelled the death knell for the disco era.

Willow and I met at the outset of our freshman year when we signed up as DJs at WDPU. I had never met anyone like her. Willow introduced me to the term "contrarian sex," which she invented and defined as an intimate encounter with someone that you found so repulsive that you couldn't help but be turned on. For example, she thought Steve Dahl was a pig, but would have tattooed his name on her ass to sleep with him. So I got us tickets to see Steve Dahl and his sidekick, Garry Meier, at a record store. There we ran into a guy so creepy that the cops monitoring the event eventually asked him to leave—at the behest of several women who were waiting in line to get Dahl's autograph.

Willow didn't even get near Steve Dahl that day, but on the way home I told her that I vaguely understand the appeal of sleeping with someone famous (or regionally famous, in this case). It was then that she clarified "contrarian sex" for me.

Willow explained that the creepy guy in the record store was the spitting image of her high school guidance counselor—a balding, paunchy 40-something loser with a penchant for short-sleeve shirts and clip-on ties. His breath, she told me, matched the occasional shit stains on his pants. Willow cringed each time she was called into his office. But that didn't stop her from occasionally performing fellatio on him. She said she liked to force him to face the picture of his wife and kids that he kept on his desk while he was coming to orgasm.

The trend continued in college; the easiest way to get into her pants was to repulse her. A nubile girl with gorgeous almond eyes and a shaved head to ward off accusations of traditional beauty, her dime-store consignment clothes failed to hide the exquisite swimmer's body lurking beneath. Unfortunately, she considered me a "charming rogue," which meant that I didn't even register as a blip on her repulsion scale. I had no shot. Our common bond was music. Specifically, Pink Floyd. I thought they were overrated; she hated them.

So it was that Willow and her dueling psychosis became synonymous with *Pink Floyd*. To wit: when playing any *Pink Floyd* song on the air, she would lock the studio door, crank the studio microphone to full tilt (as opposed to the traditional muting process while a song was being played) and masturbate over the clatter.

Pink Floyd worked for her on so many levels: their songs strayed toward epic length, allowing her time to complete the arc of her sexual act; the band layered so many bizarre sounds over their tracks that a woman coming to orgasm integrated quite nicely; and, most importantly, she was repulsed by the band.

Word gets around a college campus quickly, even in the prehistoric period before Mark Zuckerberg was born. DePaul's sprawling cafeteria, which was usually a cacophony of chatter, frat boy chants and clanging silverware, came to a complete and utter hush within a few seconds of any *Pink Floyd* song queuing up during her shift.

The silence did not last long. The choir of dissonance was reconstructed in the form of loud cheers from the males and giggly, staged disbelief from the female co-eds. Roger Waters undoubtedly would have been tickled pink, so to speak, to know that the standing ovations his studio albums received at DePaul rivaled those of his live concerts anywhere on the planet.

Pitted against a legend, I didn't even bother to play *Pink Floyd* on my weekend show.

As bizarre musical memories go, however, Willow's self-strumming finished a distant second to an event that occurred nearly three decades later.

* * *

The Swell Season is, for all intents and purposes, a band of two. Irish guitarist and vocalist Glen Hansard and Czech pianist Marketa Irglova played unlikely bandmates and lovers in the brilliant 2007 film *Once*, which launched a life-imitates-art collaboration of both the musical and romantic variety. Touring together cured the latter affliction, but they kept performing as a duet when Hansard wasn't touring with his regular band, *The Frames*.

I had already seen *The Swell Season* in concert a couple of times when Sue and I slipped out of town on a Friday afternoon in August 2009 with plans to start a weekend on the Santa Cruz peninsula with the band's concert at the Mountain Winery in Saratoga.

Like the stars of the show, Sue and I had cycled through the love phase, inflicted some mutual damage and had settled into a comfortable friendship. Being a year older than me, Sue was a decisive outlier on my romantic résumé. She was tall and charmingly clumsy and way too introspective for me in the long run, but I loved her passionately until that no longer served either of our purposes.

Normally, irascible traveler was my role to play. But it was Sue who showed not the slightest bit of patience as we steered through the brutality of Friday evening Bay Area traffic. Despite the fact that we were driving right by our quaint motel on the edge of Saratoga en route to the concert, Sue became uncharacteristically agitated when I suggested stopping by the office to grab our key. I knew that we wouldn't return from the corkscrewed hill leading from the mountaintop venue until 11 p.m. or so. Having stayed at the Saratoga Oaks Lodge for several other concerts, I knew that the middle-aged couple who ran the establishment would be none too pleased to be roused at that time of night for a check-in.

The logic of my argument only served to further irritate her; Sue wanted to get to the concert venue post-haste. It is the only time I can remember her not erring on the side of consideration or compassion. I was so thrown off by her stance that I simply bit my lip as we drove past the motel. It was, in retrospect, the first sign that the evening was not going to follow form.

We grabbed our seats—sixth row, dead center stage—and settled in for a truly unforgettable show.

Even if you're not into the particular brand of hard-edged folk that defines the Swell Season, it's hard to escape the gravitational pull of Glen Hansard. There is no flash to his performances, just true grit. It's easy enough to speculate, had music not been his gift, that he might have been a longshoreman. During the warm-up band's performance that night, he sat, inconspicuously, in a seat at the end of the first row, a wool cap pulled over his unruly red locks and sweat glistening off his bushy red beard. He was smiling broadly, moving his head to the beat and intently absorbing the music as a fan.

He brings that joy and intensity to every song of every performance, like a pitcher determined to clock 100 m.p.h. on every delivery. I can only imagine the perpetual state of angst among his management team, wondering which song will be the one to implode his vocal cords.

He did not deserve what was about to befall him. Nor did Marketa Irglova, the librarian-quiet yin to her bandmate's yang. Early in the evening, after leaving the stage to don a sweater in the chill of the advancing night, something she claimed she had never done in mid-performance, Marketa made the prescient comment to the audience that she would always remember that night.

Indeed. All of us would.

At 10 p.m., about two hours into the concert, Sue was squirming. She turned to me to let me know that she was going to make a run for the bathroom after the song in progress was finished. We were so close to the stage that we thought it rude to exit during the performance. I let her know I needed to make a pit stop, too. When violin player Colm Mac Con Iomaire's intense solo was finished, we excused ourselves to the 15 people between us and the aisle and bolted up the walkway. The bathrooms were near-empty, and we met in the common area between them just a minute or two later. As she turned to head back down the aisle, I grabbed her arm. "This concert's going to be over in 20 minutes or so," I said, knowing that Mountain Winery concerts ended by 10:30 because of a local noise ordinance. "So we can either ask 15 people to let us through to our seats again, or we can just enjoy the view from here."

The plaza afforded a comprehensive view of the intimate venue, so Sue readily agreed. The band launched into one of our favorite songs. As they played the last chords, the audience exploded with appreciation. Even from afar, I could see Glen's eyes tear up. He was living the dream and living the moment, exchanging a torrent of energy with his fans. This, I was thinking, will go down as one of my favorite concert moments.

Sue turned to say something to me, but she saw only horror on my face.

In the split second she diverted her attention from the stage, I caught a peripheral view of something that I could not readily identify, but knew it to be bad—a series of snapshots, in my mind's eyes, of a shadowy figure as it progressed, incrementally, from the top of the four-story façade of a Paul Masson Winery behind the stage to the stage itself. The wallop of something landing next to Glen Hansard followed.

In my panic to assimilate the facts, a hundred scenarios ebbed and receded in the time it took Sue, now facing me, to say "What's wrong?" I grabbed her tight, perhaps to protect her from seeing what I was seeing over her shoulder. At least until I had processed what had happened.

But her instincts told her that the answer to her question was behind her. She pulled away and wheeled around just as Glen grabbed the microphone and stammered his last word to the audience: "Medic!"

As the crowd began assimilating their bits of information and the security force hastily surrounded the band and escorted them backstage, a nervous murmur overtook the Mountain Winery.

As the stage emptied, I spotted the body.

"Oh God, no," I said to Sue, gripping her arm as tightly as a baby would its mother in its first excursion into a swimming pool. "The violin player's dead!"

The spinning wheel in my mind had come to a halt on a horrific scenario: it had not been a person I'd seen, but one of the massive speakers hanging from the scaffolding above the stage. It had come unhinged and crashed atop Colm Mac Con Iomaire, mere feet from Glen Hansard.

I fought an overwhelming urge to vomit.

But as I babbled out the details of my account, I caught the eye of a woman a few yards away. "I don't think that's what happened," she said to me. "I saw a guy get a running start on the roof and jump."

A few others in our section concurred. Thus did the true details start to emerge.

The *San Jose Mercury News* identified the jumper as a 32-year-old man who was attending the concert while out of jail on $150,000 bail. On the previous New Year's Eve, the paper said, he had been arrested after allegedly tying up his ex-girlfriend and threatening her life, for several hours, with a loaded shotgun. He had relented at some point, according to the article, and let her go; she had gone directly to the police. The defendant was due in court in early October, less than two months after the concert, to face the music. But he had other plans.

Now, he lay dead or dying on the stage of the

Mountain Winery before 2,000 witnesses.

Despite the unfathomable nature of the act, the facts brought me instant relief. The Gaelic violinist was backstage with the rest of the band. The figure below was either somebody who had massively overindulged and made some very bad decisions, or some selfish asshole who wanted to bring down the curtain on his final act in the grandest of manners. Either way, I immediately knew that while I would never forget what had happened, I wouldn't be haunted by it.

Sue is an upstate New York native who was pre-assembled for California. She practiced Reiki, an alternative medicine of sorts in which one supposedly exchanges energy with the patient through the palms. As a Californian, I've learned not to dismiss anything offhand. Even my mother, whom I would have put at the top of my list of those least likely to believe in any form of Eastern healing, became a staunch believer in Reiki after receiving some treatments while she was undergoing chemotherapy.

In any case, Sue considered herself quite intuitive about matters of the spirit, and she went to work on a diagnosis of the show-stopper who was slumped upon the stage before a captive audience. We were captive because the folks at Mountain Winery, in a decision they undoubtedly came to regret, made an announcement requesting everyone to stay put—their logic being that the emergency crews headed up the mountain from Saratoga didn't need to fight a traffic jam in the parking lot.

So we were all treated to an overtime version of the horror show being played out on stage, where a doctor who happened to be attending the concert was working up quite a sweat frantically performing CPR. Meanwhile, the venue's security staff shifted around in an unsuccessful attempt to shield the body from all angles of sight in the amphitheater.

"He wants to leave," Sue said, her diagnosis complete.

"Yeah, the suicide attempt sorta led me to the same conclusion," I said.

She shot me a look and continued. "He wants to leave and he's irritated that those guys are trying to make him stay."

"Baby," I replied, "he found the door a while ago. Zed's dead. This is all for show. If there weren't 2,000 people watching, they would have thrown a tarp over him 20 minutes ago."

Sue vehemently disagreed. So began one of our more absurd debates. We were finally interrupted by another announcement. With no sirens within earshot a half hour after the incident, logic finally prevailed among the decision-makers on the staff. We were asked to clear the amphitheater and wait on the plaza for the emergency crews to arrive.

By then, however, I was wed to my stance that the jumper had died as soon as he'd hit the stage and was looking for evidence to present to Sue. I crept forward on the plaza to steal a glimpse into the bowl below, convinced that the good doctor would throw in the towel as soon as the last member of the audience was out of sight.

"Sir," a security guard said to me, "would you please step back?"

The absurdity of his request struck a chord, as if I was going to see something I hadn't been forced to watch for the past 30 minutes. The sarcastic prick within emerged.

"Do you think the band's coming out for an encore?" I asked him.

After finally arriving, the EMT crew spent more than an hour at the venue, fueling Sue's argument that the jumper's mortal coil didn't unwind until later in the proceedings. I insisted that they simply had no reason to hurry, seeing as how they were merely there as undertakers. Indeed, they left with a corpse, but it was edging on midnight before they collected their grim harvest. We were among the last of the hundreds of vehicles following the flashing lights of the ambulance down the mountain. As soon as we got a cell signal, Sue's phone blew up with voicemail messages.

"I wonder who would be calling this late?" she said, failing to recognize the single number that had left a litany of messages. I didn't even attempt to hide my smugness as Sue turned on her phone's speaker and played a series of increasingly agitated messages from the couple running the motel, wondering when we would be picking up our keys.

"You know the freakiest part of all this?" she asked as we approached sea level.

"You want me to start with A or work my way backwards from Z?" I replied.

"It was the song they had just finished playing when he jumped," she said.

My eyes opened widely. "You're right," I said. "The hairs on my neck are going to stand up every time I hear it."

With that, I cued up *The Swell Season* CD we'd been listening to on the way up the mountain.

As we turned onto Pierce Road and headed toward the lights of Saratoga, Sue began to softly weep as we let the night's events wash over to the accompaniment of a song which we would never hear the same way again: "When Your Mind's Made Up."

14

The Prodigal and the Doppelgänger

With a summit that rises 3,864 feet above sea level, Mount Diablo isn't even the highest peak in the San Francisco Bay Area. That honor goes to Mount Hamilton, which reaches 4,367 feet and lays claim to the first permanent mountainside observatory in the nation, Lick Observatory.

In fact, there are hundreds of mountains in California which peak at higher altitudes than Mount Diablo. But none offer more expansive views. From the top of Diablo, according to the California Department of Parks and Recreation, you can see more of the Earth's surface than from all but one other location on the planet: the summit of Tanzania's Mount Kilimanjaro, which rises 19,341 feet above the flat Serengeti.

There is some debate about the validity of Diablo's claim on such remarkable sightlines. But the mountain unquestionably occupies a unique niche, geologically and geographically.

While the Bay Area is a superhighway of modern and ancient earthquake fault lines, they are generally of the strike-slip variety, in which adjacent plates give in to pressure and one slides upward along the other. Diablo, however, appears to have been formed by a much more violent tectonic episode; her southwestern face is scarred by a thrust fault that essentially flipped the fossilized sediments from several geological eras; while logic dictates that geologic rock should be stacked with the newer atop the older, the peak of Mount Diablo consists of ancient oceanic rocks from the Jurassic and Cretaceous periods, eras that covered the arc of dinosaur life on this planet.

Geographically, Mount Diablo is unquestionably the Bay Area's most iconic promontory, recognizable for up to hundreds of miles away for its double-pyramid peak (whereas the higher Mount Hamilton blends into the Santa Cruz range). Mount Diablo was perhaps the single most important focal point for surveyors during the mapping of California. Diablo is certainly positioned for distant gazing: to the west the land slopes downward toward the San Francisco Bay; to the east lies the flat farmland of the central San Joaquin Valley, all the way to the foothills of the Sierra Nevada range.

I was captivated by the snow-covered peaks of the distant Sierra on my very first hike to Diablo, where I was introduced to the pastime.

I have returned to her trails again and again, not only because they provide the Bay Area's most rigorous training for more ambitious day-hikes, like Yosemite National Park's signature trek to Half Dome, but because I have long been drawn by Diablo's mysticism.

The mythology of two Native American tribes, the Miwoks and Ohlones, honored Diablo as the point of creation. So sacred was her peak that tribesman, serving as guides to Spanish explorers when they weren't fighting them, refused to accompany white men to Diablo's upper reaches.

They would be disheartened to learn that the peak is now a parking lot, accessible, in much the same manner as Yosemite's breathlessly beautiful Glacier Point, by combustible engine. Transforming sacred places into tourist destinations isn't strictly an American venture, of course; ask anyone who has hiked to Machu Picchu and then had to Photoshop their pictures to mask the garbage deposited by those who took the train.

The highest point on Diablo's summit is a beacon tower built by Standard Oil at the outset of World War II for the purposes of aerial navigation. Its piercing light once was visible across thousands of square miles. Today, it is illuminated but once a year, on December 7, to mark each anniversary of Pearl Harbor.

After a solo hike up the whole of the mountain from the town of Clayton in November 2006, I was relaxing on the observation deck when a man who was the spitting image of my father walked out of the tiny museum on the first floor of the building. I was riveted to his every action for several minutes as he circumnavigated the sidewalk bordering the parking lot, taking in the magnificent view and peering into the coin telescopes. He not only looked like my dad, but shared his distinctive gait and wore similar glasses. Against all logic, I became convinced that it was my Dad. I rushed down the back stairs leading from the observation deck to the parking level, hoping not to lose sight of him among the throngs.

It took a minute, but I finally spotted him conversing with a biker who was in the process of re-filling his water bottle. Having just refilled the Camelback bladder in my backpack from the same fountain 10 minutes earlier, I fished around my pack for a prop and came up with an empty Gatorade bottle. I excused myself and stepped between them on the premise of filling it.

The two men parted to allow me access to the fountain and issued polite salutations—in German. The elder man shared my father's melancholy eyes, as well as the other remarkable physical similarities I had observed from 15 feet higher.

"It is a thirsty day, *ja?*" he said in broken English, eyeing my sweat-drenched shirt. "*Ja, es ist,*" came my equally broken response, which represented virtually my entire harvest from a German class that I took twice in college.

I hadn't noticed that my hands were a bit shaky with emotion until my bottle grew heavy and I dropped it, spilling water under the wheels and feet of the biker. Having virtually exhausted my German vocabulary, I apologized in English.

Although graceless exits run counter to my personality, I could not fight the overwhelming urge to leave. I screwed the top on the bottle without any attempt to refill it—I didn't really need it, after all. The Germans said something that I didn't understand, but it was undoubtedly some sort of kindness, as in "please fill your water bottle."

But my vision was rapidly blurring, so I slid my sunglasses into position and sprang to my feet without lifting my head. I wheeled around and headed away from them, raising my hand and pulling the last reserves from my German class(es) a quarter century earlier. "*Auf Wiedersehen!*" I shouted as I found the trail and began the downhill plunge without a backward glance.

From out of nowhere, my eyes had welled up and tears were streaking down my face. I missed my dad, who had turned 70 a few months earlier.

Two weeks later, my hastily planned flight home morphed into a caustic chain of events. It started with me sprinting to the top of the steps at the BART station in Oakland only to have the doors slam in my face as I reached the platform. I was three seconds late. The next train was just three minutes away, but, in typical fashion, I had built in no margin for error. At the San Francisco airport, my mad dash to the gate ended with the ramp doors being sealed—once again, in my face. It was a week before Thanksgiving and I was holding what amounted to a stand-by ticket—a "buddy pass" issued by my best friend from college, Scott Davis, who had grown up to be a captain for Frontier Airlines. I already knew I had no chance of getting on the next flight, which was overbooked. So I spent nine hours in the airport before getting airborne.

Next was Frontier's mandatory stop in Denver, its national hub, where I realized that the final leg of my flight would put me in Dayton after the rental car counters had shuttered for the evening. The plan was to surprise my parents, so my sister Erin was the only one aware of my flight plans. Although Dayton and my hometown of Columbus are just 70 miles apart, there's no way I would have asked her to make that round trip in the middle of the night, especially when she had to work the next day. Our dad would have gladly done it, but I was determined not to ruin the surprise.

I had no intention of spending the night in Dayton, so I checked the board and discovered a flight to Indianapolis leaving an hour after the Dayton flight. Landing in Indy would add another 100 miles to my drive, but the rental car counters stayed open late. Landing at last, I waited in line for 30 minutes at the rental car counter, only to be told that my membership card allowed me to go straight to the lot and pick out the car of my choice. But after picking out a car and driving to the check-out shack, my credit card didn't match the long-since expired card I had apparently used to open the account years earlier. The mess took another half-hour to sort out, with me re-enrolling using a different credit card.

By the time I completed the three-hour drive, it was 4 a.m.: 19 hours, door-to-door. I could have flown to Spain. All of the madness was for want of an extra three seconds at the BART station in Oakland.

When Erin roused me a few hours later, I was still fully clothed, with one shoe on, face down on the bed in her spare room and fermenting in my own drool. She was leaving for work, and since our plan called for me to surprise our dad when he was making his ritualistic morning walk with Erin's dog, Seamus, I had to be out of the house shortly after she left.

I stumbled into the shower and even drank some coffee, which usually isn't my thing—I come pre-caffeinated—but was still punch drunk when I left the house. I had nowhere in particular to go, but had to lie low, because my brother Patrick and his wife, Julie, lived in the neighborhood along with their two kids, Ian and Meghan. None of them were supposed to know that I was in town just yet.

Fortunately, Dad was a man of precision. He was due at the house at 9 a.m., which meant that I could count on him arriving somewhere between 8:59 and 9:01. To play it safe, I left at 8:30. I was in no danger of Dad recognizing my rental car, so I decided to leave it parked in front of Erin's place and stretch my legs. The cemetery across the street, where I spent countless dozens of hours in high school, was calling to me.

Graveyards have held my fascination for as long as I can recall. As kids, my cousins and I wandered the vast acreage of Green Lawn Cemetery, forever searching for the graves of the locally famous: Brigadier General James Forsyth, who commanded the troops at the Battle of Wounded Knee; World War II flying ace Eddie Rickenbacker; and Columbus' most noted literary son, James Thurber.

By contrast, Wesley Chapel Cemetery, across the street from my sister's house and a few hundred yards down the road from my parents' place, was tiny, just a handful of acres. But its oldest section predated even Green Lawn. Tucked between a small chapel and the hedges lining a dangerous curve on Dublin Road are the graves of Civil War survivors and their families. As a teen, I used to jog along the Scioto River and conclude my runs in the cemetery, futilely searching the fading headstones for a 200-year old grave.

Thinking my odds might be better in 2006 than they were in the 1970s, I renewed my search while I waited for my dad to show up—I would be able to spot his car turning onto my sister's street from my vantage point in the bone yard. Sure enough, I found a tombstone dated 1803. Upon it was etched a religious imploration of some kind, but most of the words had been eroded by time, so that only three were still legible " … JESUS, OH JESUS …," with the first two words on the line above the latter.

A few days later, I brought my 11-year-old nephew Ian to the site—inexplicably, he had never been to the cemetery, although it was a mere three minutes from his house by bike. When I showed him my find, he looked puzzled. Tracing his finger along the first line, "JESUS, OH" he looked up at me and asked, "Where's Jesus, Ohio?"

I laughed so hard I developed hiccups, and Ian, although he didn't know why, was soon caught up in the hysteria. That will always be one of my favorite memories of my nephew, the two of us, rolling on the leaf-strewn ground among the long interred, laughing until our lungs ached in the crisp November air.

In the terror-based Catholicism of my youth, I would have considered our conduct that day an act of sacrilege. But over the years, I have come to regard cemeteries like redwood forests: living caretakers of the past in whose presence I am most aware of my mortality, and therefore the most celebratory of the here and now. I believe it to be a two-way street; I have little doubt that those who have walked before me—be it John Muir on a mountain trail or the woman who was reposed six feet beneath me—appreciate the mirthful sounds of life.

It wouldn't be the last time on that trip that Ian would double me over at Wesley Chapel Cemetery. He enjoyed his inaugural excursion so much that we went back in search of a grave from the 18th century. On the short ride, he told me that his friend's dad, a 34-year-old who died of an embolism after returning from a jog, was recently buried there. He asked if we could visit his grave. When I asked where it was, Ian said he didn't know, exactly, but it should be easy to find.

"How do you figure?" I asked.

"Because they're buried in alphabetical order, aren't they?" Ian replied.

I had yet to discover Ian's penchant for graveyard comedy as I waited for my father to arrive at my sister's place. At 9 a.m. on the button, I spotted his car turning onto Brookview Lane. I waited a few minutes to allow him to collect Seamus, an unwieldy Australian Shepherd pup that Erin brought home two months earlier, just a month after she was forced to put down her beloved Shep, another Aussie Shepherd that outlasted her marriage. Seamus, who was already as tall as the fire hydrants he loved to terrorize, lived in a cage during his formative months (lest he destroy my sister's condo) and required twice-daily walkings.

I was standing a few doors down, tying to look inconspicuous, when my dad emerged with Seamus, who was already trying to escape the bonds of his leash. Seamus' favorite game was attempting to dislocate the arm of his handler, and the larger he grew, the more jarring it became for all who attempted to keep him at leash's end. The last time our mother attempted the feat, one of Seamus' Iditarod-caliber thrusts pulled her to the ice, breaking her hand.

I had no trouble sneaking up on my dad as he was trying to get a handle on the pup.

"Mr. Higgins?" I said to the man I hadn't seen in over two years. "Yes," he said, turning his head and peering over his glasses, a pose in which he will live in memoriam for me. "How are you sir," I said, extending a hand. "I'm your oldest son."

"For God's sake," he said as we embraced, "Where did you come from?" Those damned Mount Diablo tears welled up again. And they had nothing to do with the fact that I was being mauled by a psychotic Australian Shepherd.

I unraveled the tale of my harrowing journey as we walked the Scioto River trail of my youth. Truth be told, I timed my visit to coincide with the greatest rivalry in all of sports—the Ohio State-Michigan football game—which would take place the next day at Ohio Stadium, less than 10 miles from where we were standing. That year marked an historic meeting in college football's most celebrated rivalry: Both teams were undefeated: Ohio State was ranked No. 1 in the nation; Michigan was No. 2. Even along the sleepy Scioto River, the air was electric. Our conversation quickly turned to the game.

About midway between my sister's place and the Fishinger Road Bridge, as Seamus was shaking off his foray into the Scioto and baptizing us with cold, stinky river water, I decided to give Dad a break and take over leash duty. Seamus exploited the change-over by bolting for the rock wall separating the park from the private residences on the wooded hillside above it. He cleared the wall in a single bound and began closing in on a man raking his lawn, barking incessantly all the way.

We were screaming at Seamus to return to the public side of the wall, but the bearded man waved a hand at us. "That's all right," he said, "let him run!" He gave Seamus a few perfunctory pats on the head as he ran by, jumping and foraging in what had seconds earlier been tidy piles of leaves. The man traversed the hill and met us by the wall. "Really sorry about that," Dad said. "Don't give it a second thought," the man replied, "I have two of them, and it's best to let them run themselves ragged."

"I'm not sure we've found this one's ragged point yet," Dad said of Seamus.

The man held out his hand and introduced himself, as Midwesterners are prone to do. California has a played-out reputation as the laid-back capital of the world. But compared with the Midwest, there is little sense of community. In Columbus, the Buckeyes unite all—young and old, men and women, Republicans and Democrats, the affluent and the poor, ethnicity and education be damned.

After the introductions, the man got straight to the

point. "Did you guys hear about Bo?" he asked.

In Columbus, ground zero of enemy territory, legendary former Michigan coach Bo Schembechler needed no last name.

My dad and I shook our heads.

"Bo died this morning," he said. "Can you believe it?"

We could not. On the eve of the most storied game in the history of the nation's most storied rivalry, the coach synonymous with Michigan football had somehow thickened a plot that needed no stirring.

As we returned to Erin's place, even Seamus seemed subdued by the sensationally timed news.

With Dad and Erin keeping mum about my arrival in town, the entire clan met up at Patrick J's, the campus-area bar where my youngest sibling, Dennis, holds court year-round, the Norm Peterson of north campus. A pub-sized faction of Ohio State's renowned band—officially named The Best Damn Band In The Land (in the same spirit of humility as the school officially calling itself *The* Ohio State University)— showed up to entertain for nearly an hour. That's akin to U2 dropping into a pub in Dublin to knock out a set. In the midst of the celebration, I casually strolled in, much to the shock of my other siblings, in-laws, several relatives and assorted cronies from as far back as high school. Perhaps the most surprised was my mother, who was in remission from battles with breast and colon cancer. She gave me a lingering hug while simultaneously commandeering the distressed, overwhelmed waitress to take my drink order.

It was an occasion for the ages; the photographs from that night depict our family at its most joyous, frozen in perpetuity in Scarlet and Gray.

I didn't have tickets to the game, a privilege extended to a mere 105,000 people. But by the time the evening ended at Patrick J's, my brother—another Patrick J(oseph)—had secured the next best thing: a spot for me at one of the lavish, elaborately organized tailgate parties that extended like spokes from the stadium, encompassing hundreds of thousands of additional fans.

Ohio State tailgate parties were no poor-man's Plan B, especially during Michigan week. Tailgate spaces rented at a premium and the collectives that ran them—in this case, a group of friends from Patrick's church—invested tens of thousands of dollars in generators, big-screen TVs, weatherproofing, heating units, decorations, heating trays, furniture, kegs, liquor and food. Most of the tailgates were worth the price of cars, some of them of the luxury class, and they proliferated as far as the eye could see.

I counted more than 70 such camps just in the parking lot that we occupied outside Ohio State's Fawcett Center. And there were similar lots running down Olentangy River Road all the way to the stadium, which after nightfall appeared as a mere dome of light in the distance. It was bitterly cold that day, but nobody cared. I could easily imagine the governor declaring a state of emergency under similar meteorological circumstances in California.

The Wolverines scored first, prompting a cute blonde co-ed fully attired in Michigan gear to stroll into our tent and ask everyone in sight, in feigned innocence, "What just happened?" It was Patrick, he of the gallows humor, who turned her away with directions to "go bury your dead." After she staggered out, he turned to me with a prediction: "Ten to one they find her in the Olentangy River without her pants tomorrow."

Indeed, the day did not end well for her. The Buckeyes won an epic battle, 42-39, and our frozen lot was transformed into Nirvana. As proof that the fortunes of the state and the Buckeyes are inexorably linked, the Pick Four in that night's Ohio Lottery was 4-2-3-9. There were 401 winners, each claiming $5,000.

In the long run, it didn't end well for the Buckeyes, either. Or me, for that matter. High on my Columbus experience, I paid $1,100 for a seat in the student section of the end zone to watch Ohio State get prison-raped, 41-14, by Florida in the national championship game in Glendale, Arizona seven weeks later.

But before leaving Columbus, I celebrated what turned out to be my final Thanksgiving with my parents; I returned to town several more times before their near-simultaneous deaths in 2011, but we were never again united for the holidays. During Thanksgiving dinner, my brother Dennis mentioned the band INXS as the answer to a trivia question which yielded him some concert tickets from a radio station. We all nearly choked on our turkey when Mom, with her 10- and 7-year-old grandchildren at the table, blurted out: "Oh, that's the band with the guy who died of autoerotic asphyxiation," referring to lead singer Michael Hutchence's death-by-masturbation in a London hotel room nine years earlier.

The apples in the Higgins family had not fallen far from the tree.

As the stories flowed, I slowly looked around the table at three generations of the Higgins family. Our mother, beautiful in her youth, had been ravaged by her battles with cancer and was gaunt, but still took fierce pride in her appearance, dying her hair and meticulously applying her make-up. Two years earlier, the strongest woman I had ever known collapsed in my arms, bald as a baby from chemotherapy, and cried herself to sleep in fits and spasms. A man loses his innocence in all sorts of ways. The last of mine took flight that day.

Our dad, ever in command of turkey carving, still sported a full head of salt-and-pepper hair at 70. He still was quick with a smile, as well, but the melancholy that had always been present in his sleepy brown eyes had become more prevalent, as if on heightened scrutiny for any invaders who might try to penetrate the walled perimeters of his heart. I recognized in that moment my own internal alerts against intimacy and wondered if the system could be disarmed or, like DNA, was simply hard-wired.

But it was a sense of prevailing peace that ruled the day. My parents had raised four relatively well-adjusted children, all with delightfully warped senses of humor, and now had the means and the time to dote on two grandchildren who, much to their delight, often terrorized their own parents. Payback was a bitch.

Catholicism and Buckeye-ism were but two-thirds of the Shamrock of Absolute Truths into which the Higgins children and grandchildren were indoctrinated at birth. The other irrefutable fact of our existence was that we were 100 percent Irish, our blood undiluted by pagan empires (which was all of them outside the Emerald Isle).

Ultimately, the entire triumvirate proved fallible.

While passing time on my laptop in the Denver airport on the considerably less dramatic journey back to California, I clicked on an ad for a trial subscription to Ancestry.com. After a few days, I had pieced together a sizable representation of four generations of my family. Much to my horror, there was blood from the Fatherland in our veins. There, among my maternal great-grandparents, was Anna Kroninbitter, who immigrated to the U.S. from Germany, lineage of which my mother surely must have been aware.

I flashed back to my encounter with my father's doppelgänger atop Mount Diablo a few weeks earlier, and once again bowed my head in humility to my explorer-hero, John Muir, who admonished that all things are "hitched to everything else in the universe."

15

Mountain Orgy

I was hiking on Mount Tamalpais, which rises dramatically from the ocean floor north of the Golden Gate Bridge, when one of my regular trail partners halted in mid-step. "You've got to be kidding me!" she exclaimed in her most accusatory tone.

We were dating but in the process of uncoupling, so my brain instinctively began scanning for infractions and lapses in judgment I might have committed during the previous 24 hours. Finding none, I was in the process of reviewing the previous week when she added a clue.

"I can't believe you make a living as a trained observer," she said of my occupation as a journalist. "Did you not see that?"

"See what?"

"That," she said, taking me by the shoulders and spinning me 180 degrees.

There, not 10 feet from the bend we just rounded,

was an old man, as naked as a jaybird, alternately washing his armpits and saggy testicles in some seasonal runoff that created a small waterfall for the first few months of most years.

He waved amicably.

"You missed a spot," my soon-to-be-ex-girlfriend said to him, pointing to her derriere to direct his efforts.

He waved again in appreciation.

As Simon & Garfield noted in *The Boxer*, "a man hears what he wants to hear and disregards the rest." The same apparently applied to sight, for while my job reviews from editors were generally favorable in the areas of writing and reporting, I was eternally grateful that there was no category entitled "powers of observation."

It provided an endless source of amusement and irritation to my colleagues. It wasn't uncommon for me, while sitting in the press box of a football stadium, to miss what was right in front of me. On one not atypical occasion during a Cal blowout loss in Berkeley, I was scanning the hills of Strawberry Canyon for a metaphor to work into my article. I was fixated on a pack of seabirds dive-bombing the prematurely emptying stadium when a roar went up from the dissipating crowd. "What just happened?" I'd asked of my fellow reporters from competitive media outlets.

"Blocked field goal. Returned it 77 yards for a touchdown," came the reply. The unspoken "you idiot" was assumed.

I blame genetics. Even Erin, my mature and responsible sibling, was not immune to the elusive nature of reality. When visiting from the flatlands of Ohio one summer, I took her on her first hike on

A GOOD LOOK BEFORE DARK

Mount Tam. As we hit the summit and began the downhill trek, she stopped to read the detailed signs warning of possible encounters with mountain lions and rattlesnakes.

Not a minute had passed before I felt Erin's death grip on my arm. "Oh God," she said, as if she were going to vomit. "Th-th-there's a m-m-mountain lion."

I was as excited as I was nervous. For more than 10 years, I had been hiking the hills of California, itching for such an encounter. I had run across the occasional bobcat, but unless you're a rabbit, they aren't much more threatening than a house cat. And here was Erin, hitting the jackpot four miles into her first hike.

Years earlier, I set up a Google alert for "mountain lion," and read every story that flashed across my screen. I knew that encounters in California were few and far between, and they usually passed without incident. The exception generally occurred when someone panicked—which, I could feel by the fingernails digging into my arm, appeared to be a distinct possibility with my sister.

"Relax and breathe," I said. I was facing the summit and she was turned downhill, toward the ocean, so I had no idea how close the big cat was. I mentally reviewed the checklist I had memorized: No quick movements. Lock eyes. Do not retreat. Make myself appear larger, hands up, like a defender guarding the lane in basketball. Make threatening noises, if necessary. But most of all, don't let the cat smell fear.

I felt as prepared for the moment as I could be.

I rotated slowly toward the west. I could read in Erin's widening eyes that the threat was still some distance off. That was good.

As I squared my shoulders toward the trail below

us, I spotted the object of her discontent.

"Oh man," I said. "We're screwed. That's a species we didn't want to come across."

"Oh, please, no," Erin whimpered. "What is it?"

"It's Bambi's mother," I said, ripping my soon-to-be black-and-blue arm free of her grip as the doe, gentling nibbling on a bush, perked her ears in our direction. "It's a deer."

So I'm still awaiting my first mountain lion encounter. And who knows? There may be a mountain lion somewhere awaiting an encounter with me. After all, I have proven to be sweet meat in the wildlife kingdom, time and time again—specifically among insects.

Perhaps it is karma paying me back for my pre-adolescent love affair with DDT, but mosquitoes will pick me out of a pack of 30 hikers and dive-bomb me for three miles on a trail while my hiking companions give me a wide berth. I invariably serve as the gluey human fly strip for any group in which I travel.

Scientists have long studied what attracts mosquitoes and other insects to certain people. A University of Florida study declared that one in 10 people are highly attractive to female mosquitoes (males don't bite). Researchers generally agree on this: mosquitoes zero in on their human prey from long distances, as much as 150 feet away, and consider carbon dioxide and heat output a beacon for them.

Which makes sense, in my case, since I have always run hot. I am invariably the sweatiest hiker in the pack, even when I'm among the best-conditioned. I hike in shorts, even on trails with residual snow. I tend to shed all sheets and covers in my sleep, even in winter; no woman has ever complained about me hogging the covers (it's on my resumé).

Never has my insect-ual love affair been more apparent than on a summer hike along Big Sur with the same woman, a few months after the naked guy in the waterfall incident. By then we had indeed downgraded our relationship from a romantic one to a platonic one, but the transition was so gradual that neither of us inflicted any wounds upon the other. We were bound by our love of hiking.

For most of the trip, the fog line hovered 1,000 feet or higher above sea level. As we day-hiked our way south toward Ragged Point, midway between San Francisco and Los Angeles, the treks got steeper and the temperatures in the high country above the marine layer soared.

On the final day, while scaling the Junipero Serra Peak in Los Padres National Forest, surmounting the fog line provided another surprise: an orgy of black flies making the best of their very brief mating season. The smallest were the size of a dime; the largest as big as a quarter. Their bite was sharp, like a mild bee sting. My partner violently slapped away a few, applied some Cutter, and that was that. They weren't all that interested in her.

That's because I was available. By the time we reached the peak, I had been bitten hundreds of times, and rivulets of blood were flowing, in crisscrossing patterns, down both legs. I rarely travel lightly, which is why I make a much better day hiker than camper. Between the emergency first aid supplies I carry for the groups I lead, the bug sprays and poison oak remedies, multiple changes of outerwear and enough water and Gatorade to fortify a basketball team through a triple-overtime game, I wear out backpacks as often as hiking boots.

But nothing I was carrying that day tempered the appetite of the hormone-crazed bomber flies; the madder my alchemy of ointments and sprays became, the more they wanted to do to me what they were doing to each other.

Their numbers thinned as we rose higher, and they had dissipated by the time we bagged the summit. But we, or rather I, would have to negotiate their firing lines on the downhill trek. Although I wouldn't be as sweaty going downhill, it was so steep and rocky in their mating zone that I figured we might actually spend more time descending through their turf than we did climbing it. If I submitted to gravity to rush through their swarms, I might be trading the bloodletting for a broken ankle. As we say in the day-hiking biz, nobody gets hurt going uphill.

I was in the habit of changing my sweat-drenched shirt at the apex of every hike. That day, I was wearing a long-sleeved shirt made of rayon. And even as it became as wet as a pond, it had protected my arms, if not my hands, from the ravages of the orgiastic flies.

My legs, however, were raw, pocked as if from hundred rounds from a BB gun. I decided that they couldn't take any more tenderizing. So I pulled off the rayon shirt, tore it in half, and did my best to fit the pieces as leggings. I threw on a cotton shirt and hoped for the best.

Being an over-packer, I hadn't thought twice about throwing a bottle of wine into my backpack, with the idea of surprising my now-platonic partner with a celebratory libation to finish off the trip when we hit the summit. I had not, of course, had the foresight to include a corkscrew or drinking vessels. But I was determined not to let such stupidity deter the intention. So I peeled off the aluminum around the top with a pocket knife and used a stick to tamp down the cork until it rescinded, in dozens of pieces, into the bottle – which was hot to the touch inside the steamy backpack. We enjoyed a granular, boiling cabernet in alternating chugs, straight out of the bottle, before beginning the downhill trek.

It turns out that mating black flies, too, are fond of alcohol. Especially when distilled in the form of sweat. As even black flies know, the only thing better than sex is sex with a buzz. And in their pre- and post-coitus zeal to belly up to the bar, my leggings strategy was rendered moot; one by one, they simply bit through the rayon.

Back at the hotel, as I applied rubbing alcohol to what was left of the skin on my legs—as unpleasant a npost-hike exercise as I have ever endured—my hiking partner marveled at the fact that she had gone virtually unmolested while I was being skinned alive. She mused that if anyone could invent an insect repellant that worked on me, they'd be wealthier than Bill Gates.

I told her of the existence of such an elixir, one that I hadn't seen since my days as a young journalist in Savannah. She scoffed that such a product existed.

So I told her of Georgia's famed Gnat Line, which serves as a 38th paralell for one of the most annoying, persistent and celebrated insects in the country. The areas of the Peach State north of the line, including Atlanta, are unaffected. South of the Gnat Line, it's everyone for himself.

Milledgeville, located roughly in the middle of a triangle formed by Atlanta, Macon and Augusta, holds a Gnat Days Festival every year. There may be no more appropriately named sports franchise in the nation than Savannah's minor-league baseball team, the Sand Gnats. The city's outlying marshes are gnat bordellos.

Individually, gnats are practically unnoticeable. But they travel in packs, often numbering in the millions, as thick as smoke. Which means that during the hottest months of the year, outdoor enthusiasts are exposed not only to Savannah's searing heat and wretched humidity, but roaming black clouds of gnats steeped in Kamikaze tradition.

Their aerial circuses are a thing to behold. It is possible, when they are gathered in sufficient numbers, to see them coming from a few hundred yards away, a distance they can close in mere seconds. They are equally impressive at putting on the brakes when they make contact with humans. Their general orders are to conduct psychological warfare, hovering and annoying more than attacking. But with numbers so prolific, a few make their way into moist openings of the eyes, nose and mouth.

But with me, they didn't hesitate to attack any exposed opening in my body. I often swallowed or inhaled as many as I could spit or blow out. While covering high school baseball games for the *Savannah Morning News* in the late 1980s, I packed a small mirror, saline solution and an extra pair of Bausch & Lombs in my computer bag, because the most ambitious of gnats could limbo underneath my contact lenses.

There was no bug repellent that remotely waylaid them in the completion of their duties. Their only known Kryptonite was a feminine beauty product: a moisturizer distributed by Avon called Skin So Soft.

In three years in Savannah, I could count on two hands the number of girls and women of whom I inquired who did not carry Skin So Soft, often mixed with water in a spray bottle. And though Southern men wear their machismo on their sleeves, the skin not covered by sleeves was liberally covered in Skin So Soft.

I knew women who significantly augmented their family income selling just one Avon product. But the ultimate testimony to the product's efficacy might be this: It even worked on me.

On that day among the black flies in Los Padres National Forest, I would have given a month's salary for a bottle of the magical elixir.

My partner, upon hearing the story, whelped with delight, spitting out pieces of the Clif Bar she was consuming while we awaited room service. She ran to her backpack and dumped the contents.

Onto the bed, right beside a bag of almonds and a pair of tweezers, spilled a bottle of Skin So Soft.

16

The Angel of Death

I just happened to be headed into town when Herbie Commeans dropped dead from a heart attack at 58.

If the carnage had been limited to Herbie, the brother my father never had, nobody would have suspected a thing. But the bodies of relatives and family friends seemed to be piling up around my visits to my hometown of Columbus, Ohio. I'd book a flight, and somebody's days became numbered.

My mother was the first to spot the trend.

"You know what you are?" she said after scanning the obituaries during one of my visits. "You're the Angel of Death."

Some might have been insulted. I was awestruck.

I began to ponder if I might be able to apply my omnipotent powers intentionally, rather than randomly.

Mom interrupted the fantasy when she suggested that the Angel of Death was going to have a hard time getting past the Pearly Gates ... especially since he didn't attend Mass. That was my cue to walk away. I tried to steer clear of religious discussions with my mother. She was devout and I was not, and it never ended well.

But Catholic funerals tended to reignite an old debate. Mom was adamant in her belief that a priest was the only person fit to deliver a eulogy, come hell or high water. I thought the task was best suited, on more occasions than not, to family or friends.

In fact, I considered myself an expert on the subject, having spent my pre-adolescent Sundays as an altar boy at St. Thomas the Apostle.

The only time altar boys received any earthly remuneration was in the form of a tip from the family of someone who was being married or buried, so I was constantly badgering Monsignor Eastadt and Father Durst to sign me up for nuptials and funerals. By the time I was a teenager, I had suffered through as many eulogies as the average 85-year-old.

The parish priests weren't always familiar with the dearly departed. Some so-called parishioners only attended Mass on holidays, others only in their own coffin. Then there were the times when the priests knew plenty about the deceased, but protocol prevented them from using terms like "petty asshole" in their summations. Thus were saints and sinners, losers and winners often lumped into the same eulogy template. The altar boys on the regular rotation kept themselves awake with small-change wagering on which adjectives the priest would use most frequently, with "devoted" and "family-oriented" among the best investments.

As Herbie was being laid to rest, we kicked up the dust on our old disagreement, but Mom would not be swayed by my expertise. She threatened, on numerous occasions, to haunt me for eternity if anyone but a man of the cloth uttered a word at her funeral. She wasn't even budged by the tragicomedy events of Herbie's funeral, when the aging priest conducting the graveside service referred to him as "Henry" a half-dozen times.

He didn't stop until Herbie's oldest daughter, Vicki, strolled to the podium and attempted to whisper a correction in his ear. "What's that?" he asked, loud enough to be heard in the back row. Vicki rolled her eyes. "His name is Herbert," she said aloud, giving up on the charade of confidentially. The old coot corrected course and got the last few references right, but the damage had been done. Another family might have been tattooed by the experience, but from a few rows back I could see Vicki, her sister and two brothers shaking with laughter. It reminded me why I'd had a crush on her as a kid. She was cute as a girl and beautiful as a woman, sarcasm and a dour view of men wrapped in humor and curves.

Vicki and I were destined to meet long before we were born. My dad was an only child, which showed remarkable reproductive restraint on the part of my grandmother, considering her multiple marriages. Scouting for her next ex-hubby, booze and Pall Mall cigarettes left Grandma with little time for mundane chores like child-rearing. Despite those handicaps, my father entered high school with excellent promise as a student and athlete. But his trajectory wasn't sustainable in his environment.

Enter Leonard and Virginia Commeans, a kindly couple whose son, Herbie, attended school with my dad at St. Thomas Aquinas High, an all-boys institution where the priests packed a punch for students who didn't toe the line. The Commeans family opened their doors to my father, rearing him as one of their own. He flourished in the classroom and was a terror on the football field, where he earned all-city honors on both sides of the ball in his junior year. As a senior, he was named a captain of the all-state team. Along the way, Dad and Herbie became brothers from different mothers.

Herbie's funeral marked the first time in 15 years I had seen Vicki. I wouldn't see her again for 15 more. In the meantime, I continued to burnish my reputation as the Angel of Death. My brother Patrick, purveyor of toilet and gallows humor, once had me paged at the Columbus airport as I was leaving town. It was just a month or so after 9/11, so the page freaked me out. I rushed to the airline's white courtesy phone, half-prepared to explain the *Playboy* I had stashed in my checked baggage.

"Hello?" I said, more of a question than a salutation.

"Hey Brian," Patrick replied. "Aunt Maureen's dead."

"Ummm, that sucks," I replied as I tried to recall the last time I'd seen Aunt Maureen. "My plane's about to board."

"Just wanted to make it official," he said. "You were still in town when it happened."

Our mother, too, was amused by the body count at first. Over time, however, she became convinced that I possessed supernatural powers to control the population of Columbus, Ohio. Chemotherapy, first for breast cancer and then for unrelated colon cancer, took a toll on her body, and her doctors told her that she would eventually need to have her heart valves replaced; Dad was fond of telling her that he was going to deposit her in a dumpster upon her next malfunction. But there seemed to be no hurry in scheduling the operation—it actually took a few years to come to fruition. When she finally did check into the hospital, the doctors delayed things further with tests for this and that. All told, she was in the hospital for 19 days, understandably going stir-crazy for much of the time.

On one of my daily calls to her room, I broached the subject of a visit.

"Oh no," she said without a trace of ambiguity, "You're close enough, right there in California."

I was at a respectful distance of 2,100 miles when she lapsed into a coma two days after being released from the hospital. She never regained consciousness. Five days later, I did my grim duty—escorting her into the hereafter from her bedside, with the help of the rest of our family, on July 3, 2011.

"I'll bet she would have preferred to die on the 2nd," our father lamented after his wife took her final breath, two hours after the respirator sustaining her was turned off. "She was born on the 2nd and married on the 2nd. That was her day."

On the way out of the hospital, my siblings and I stopped by the nurses' station to thank them for their compassion and professionalism during her stay. In plain sight was the sheet recording our mother's official time of death: 2:22 p.m.

The fog of mourning and the endless wet rituals associated with Irish send-offs blurred the days that followed, and the oppressive humidity of an Ohio July did little to evaporate the pain. On a day seared in my memory, however, I was awaiting a lift to the airport from my brother Dennis. I was ambivalent about my return to California, desperately wanting to flee but dreading taking leave of my father, whose personality had been muted overnight, a proud boxer clutching the ropes of a stunning defeat.

We had gathered as a family on the deck on which my parents had celebrated their final drink—the gin and tonics that I had forsaken in college—busy with the mindless task of writing thank-you notes to the legions of friends and family who had showed support during the funereal process. Erin, Patrick, our father, my sister-in-law Julie and I divided the task with dulled enthusiasm.

When Dennis arrived, intent on squiring me to Patrick J's for a final toast en route to the airport, I rose with trepidation for a final round of hugs. Dad was last in line. As I embraced him, I was rendered a child, hugging a father departing for a business trip to Dayton or Cleveland, shaking with fear that I would never see him again. I had vowed to remain stoic in order to allay his fears that I might not be man enough to face the grief ahead while isolated in California, but the sobs racked my body as I held my depleted father in my arms.

Two months later, he hollowly marked the 50th anniversary of his wedding. Two months after that, four months to the day after his wife passed away, Bill Higgins was gripped by a heart attack while dressing for another day of heartache. He died in the chair next to their bed.

The Angel of Death was nowhere in sight.

17

The Angel of Death Racks Up Frequent Flyer Miles

If the flight from San Francisco to Columbus when Mom was on her deathbed was interminable, the same trip four months later when Dad was laying in a funeral home was pure hell. The fuselage felt like my own coffin.

To hold it together, I pulled out my laptop and began to write my father's eulogy, knowing that the task was already in the capable hands of Father Mike Watson, whose history with my family predated his entry into the seminary. Father Mike had done a masterful job of eulogizing our mother, a generous and devout woman who seldom let an opinion die of natural causes. I inherited her obstinacy, blue eyes, insomnia and love for the written word, if little of her religious conviction.

Even after I escaped the confines of the airplane on my November trip to Ohio for Dad's funeral, I continued to cathartically peck away at my eulogy project. When I finished, it dawned on me that I had revealed a side of my father that nobody outside of our family could have known—even Father Mike, who worked for my dad in the insurance business and played in a company football league with him before he decided to take a more spiritual route.

I ran the idea of delivering Dad's eulogy past my sister and brothers, but they were rightfully resistant. From beyond the Great Divide, I could feel the weight of Mom's rebuke for even suggesting such blasphemy. She had long threatened that if anyone but a priest delivered a word at her or my father's funeral, she would haunt the offender to the grave.

My sister Erin came up with the perfect compromise: I could deliver my version of the eulogy at the Shamrock Club, site of the post-funeral gathering. No culture puts an exclamation point on a funeral like the Irish, and there was no guesswork involved in choosing the venue for either one of our parent's postscripts. Friday nights at the Shamrock Club were a Higgins family tradition. We had celebrated our mother's life at the Shamrock Club four months earlier, and that is where we would toast our father for the final time, as well. If my eulogy sucked, at least there would be alcohol.

If truth be told, Mom and Dad bickered like cellmates for half a century. Their verbal skirmishes so exhausted our father's reserves that he appeared—again, to everybody outside our immediate family—as the most laid-back guy in central Ohio, the yin to her blustery yang. Dad, being a lawyer, played his cards close to the vest; Mom's were splayed all over the table. She was endlessly baffled and frustrated by his effortless ability to attract people. Our father had a good ol' boy smile for everybody, but couldn't have cared less what most people thought of him. His indifference made him all the more appealing to the masses. Mom found the formula maddening.

She gained the upper hand, at long last, after the race had been run. So many people showed up at her wake that we had to request two extra sign-in books from the funeral home. Four months later, the same funeral home was once again packed with those paying respects to our father, if only in slightly less prolific numbers. Somewhere in the hereafter, we were quite sure, Mom was doing a victory dance as Dad rolled his eyes and stomped off in search of an easy chair.

Virtually everything about their death rituals was identical: the downtown Columbus funeral home; the visiting hours; the priest; the church; the cemetery; even the six pallbearers, including the three Higgins brothers.

Father Mike once again nailed the eulogy, in which he made note of our parents' droll tradition of sitting at opposite ends of the church: Mom up front, where she had kept a vigilant eye on me as an altar boy nearly four decades earlier; Dad in the back, where he could slip in and out without any fuss. The story perfectly captured their ambivalent relationship.

Although I had compiled prolific funereal experience as an altar boy, I was a relative novice as a pallbearer. Our father's casket was just the third I'd borne, after Herbie Commeans' and our mother's. My lack of polish was on display in the aftermath of Dad's funeral Mass. As the St. Andrew parking lot filled with mourners and the hearse warmed up for the procession to the cemetery, Father Mike stepped forward to bless the casket. It was about then that I noticed someone waving from across the parking lot. It was Vicki Commeans.

As I walked past Father Mike to talk to her, he seemed to be waving the aspergillum, the septum-like instrument which sprinkles holy water, in my direction. In actuality, he was merely pausing in mid-ceremony while blessing the casket. But I mistook his motion as an invitation to grab it and do some sprinkling of my own. The nearby mourners looked on with various degrees of bemusement. It was only upon handing the aspergillum back to the open-jawed priest that it dawned on me that I had just steamrolled across the secular-spiritual line. In less confining circumstances, Dad would have been doubled over in laughter.

He was laid to rest beside our mother in the last available plot in the "St. Patrick" section of St. Joseph Cemetery, which he had secured just four months earlier. The crowd then drifted to the Shamrock Club, a church basement which had long ago been converted to a bar and served as ground zero for Columbus' considerable Irish community.

Shamrock Club tradition dictated that the bereaved family foot the bar bill for all who gathered to toast the departed. Some cultures might view that as adding insult to injury, but it provided endless opportunities for my siblings and I to utter "let me buy you a drink!" on a Tuesday afternoon. The food provided by the Daughters of Erin Bereavement Committee, a smorgasbord of Midwest comfort food like fried chicken, deviled eggs, ham and casseroles of various origins.

Indeed, these were the best and worst of times. I would not wish bookend funerals on anyone, but there was plenty of reason to be grateful. My siblings and I were all in our 40s before we lost our parents, who had lived to be 72 and 75 and had more or less made their exit together. The Shamrock Club was filled with the incredible people who had formed the rich and intricate webs of their lives, and the stories, not to mention the taps, were flowing.

Few were closer to our parents than Diane and Larry Evans. Diane and our mother were classmates from first grade through high school graduation. They were separated by geography, then reunited for life two decades later when we moved to their side of town. Larry and our dad hit it off as though they had been lifetime friends as well, and Larry and Mom became gambling buddies. My siblings forged deep bonds with many of the nine Evans kids. An Irish-Italian cartel was born.

Diane prayed the rosary over our mother on her deathbed. And it was the Evans women who prepared and served an Italian feast for our family between the grueling visitors' shifts at the funeral home for both our parents.

My eulogy started with an anecdote about a scrapbook I found in our attic in the 1970s. It had been assembled two decades earlier by one of Dad's high school girlfriends. The yellowing newspaper articles revealed the football acclaim to which our father had scarcely alluded, typical of his utter lack of ego.

I also made mention of the Commeans family and another clan, the Mentels, who provided quarter for our father when his own mother failed to. I paid tribute to our mother for supporting Dad's uphill trek through night law school with three kids in tow (and a fourth down the road), and to our father's relentless pursuit of a better life than the one circumstance had dealt him. Then I switched gears:

"I don't think anyone would argue if I labeled our father as 'stoic.' That's another way of saying that he put everyone else's needs before his. Anybody who doubts that never saw him trying to catch a few winks of sleep in a plastic hospital chair, giving comfort to my mother through endless rounds of chemotherapy and other treatments.

A GOOD LOOK BEFORE DARK

"It was in those moments that Dad imparted on me a lesson for which I'll be forever grateful: what it truly meant to be a man. I will never regret that I seized the opportunity to tell him exactly that.

"His grandchildren, Ian and Meghan, cracked the façade of his stoicism. No sooner had he become a grandfather than the man who used to bark at me for leaving a light on began sending me emails of puppies wrestling with kittens.

"Our father revealed yet another side of himself four months ago, when he lost his wife of 50 years, our mother. Mom and Dad had their own version of The Honeymooners, taking squabbling to an art form. But at the moment her heart failed, his was broken—irrevocably, as it turned out.

"These four months, as painful as they've been, have been a gift to our family. Our father divulged the full extent of his love for all of us. As a family, we rallied around each other. We reveled in each other's company. Our conversations ended in a heretofore foreign phrase: 'I love you.'"

At that point, I lost the battle with my quivering lower lip, but I was hardly alone. I took a deep breath and gathered enough composure to make a lunge for the finish.

"So here's to you, Dad. And to you, Mom. Somewhere, Jane is raising hell about Bill being four months late with her gin and tonic. So let's raise a toast. To Bill and Jane. We'll see you soon enough. Sláinte!"

"*Sláinte!*" the crowd replied in unison, their voices and clinking glasses forming the beautiful harmony of the timeless Gaelic toast.

As I floated around the room, I was reminded of the estrogen orbit that I escaped when I left town after high school. Dad's side of the family tree was virtually leafless, but we were flush with relatives on Mom's side, where Irish-Catholic birth control was pervasive. She was the ninth of 10 kids who begat 21 children of their own, 16 of them girls. My brothers and I constituted the quorum of males in the entire generation; of my 17 cousins, 15 are female. Their collective embrace that day warmed my grieving heart.

Vicki and her mother, woefully lacking in Irish blood, were buzzed on one drink. Vicki asked how long I was going to be sticking around town. With both parents gone, there were papers to sign and so forth, so I told her I was planning to be in Ohio through Thanksgiving.

We made a pact to get together the next week at Patrick J's, the bar near Ohio State's campus where my family had gathered when I snuck into town for the Ohio State-Michigan festivities five years earlier. My brother Dennis, the Norm Peterson of Patrick J's, would naturally be holding court.

Dennis missed his calling as a stand-up comedian, an opinion shared by just about everybody who has crossed his path. He is a thinking man's Chris Farley, with whom he bears a physical resemblance and can imitate uncannily. He has a charming way of escalating the drinking pace to Spring Break standards, which is all the trickier when you're convulsing with laughter. If you think tequila burns going down, you should try regurgitating it through your nostrils. If a night with Dennis could be bottled, the pharmaceutical companies would be forming long lines, although the likelihood of overdosing would probably prevent it from getting past the FDA.

As if a night out with Dennis wasn't dangerous enough, his wife Brandy—named for the chart-topping

1972 song by one-hit wonder band *Looking Glass*—augmented the income from her real estate job by pouring drinks at Patrick J's.

It was under that perfect storm of influences that Vicki began to probe me as a recruit for some sort of self-improvement movement with which she was smitten. "That's hilarious," Dennis said to her. "Brian wouldn't join one of those unless hell froze over."

Or until the tequila at Patrick J's had run dry. That's apparently when I agreed to take a 220-mile round trip to Cincinnati with Vicki the Tuesday after Thanksgiving, the eve of my flight back to California.

I kept my word. But mere minutes into that journey, as Vicki and I merged onto Interstate 71 for our trip south, my cell phone vibrated. It was my sister. That afternoon, two weeks to the day after our father's funeral, Larry Evans had clutched his chest and informed Diane—his wife of 56 years—that he was having a heart attack. He pitched forward and died.

The Angel of Death had been scheduled to leave town the next day. Instead, I attended another funeral.

18

California's Seal of Self-Approval

California is its own brand of paradise, but you sign up for the whole warped package when you adopt the Golden State as your mailing address.

Whether your interests lie in mysticism, bead-wearing, micro-computing, tree-hugging, hiking, performance art or taking your sexuality to new frontiers in time and space, there's a place for you in California. And if you like to protest, you should send for a brochure immediately.

But nothing thrives in California's twisted garden like the self-improvement industry.

My path to enlightenment detoured through southern Ohio. Mere hours after Larry Evans was reunited with my parents in the Hereafter Lounge on Nov. 22, 2011, I arrived in Cincinnati—shell-shocked and receptive to anything that didn't resemble my life. I was the target audience for Landmark Education.

Landmark was the re-branded version of the

controversial "est" self-improvement courses started by Werner Erhard in the 1970s. Critics branded it as cultish, but there were multitudes that credited the program with pivoting their foundering lives. I knew nothing of "est" or Landmark when I arrived with Vicki in Cincinnati. I was just along for the ride.

Technically, we were there to mark Vicki's "graduation" from one of Landmark's advanced courses. Vicki wasn't much on theatrics, so she just sat there while her fellow grads paraded to the microphone, still high from their weekend of guided self-discovery and claiming all manner of breakthroughs.

It soon became obvious, however, that the program was little more than a recruiting session for attendees like me.

"Do you get a cut if they sign me up?" I whispered to Vicki as the woman with the microphone came to tears over a long-dead cat.

"Well, you don't seem happy," Vicki replied, folding her arms for emphasis.

"Yeah," I conceded, "this litany of death hasn't really stimulated my joy center like you'd think it would. You think they could fix that?"

"At least your gooey sarcastic center is still intact," she said, "so maybe they can start with that."

With that, Vicki motioned me to follow her into the hallway where—surprise—the registration tables were located. "I'll pay the $100 deposit," she said, handing her credit card to a woman with a beehive hairdo. "There's a session next month. I think this will do you a world of good."

"Save your money," I replied. "I'll be back in San

Francisco."

Vicki and the lady in the beehive hairdo shared a conspiratorial smile.

"Landmark Forums (the company's intro course) are held all over the world," the beehive lady explained, in a tone one might use with a puppy that had peed on the floor, "including San Francisco, our international headquarters for the past 40 years."

Vicki grinned and submitted her American Express. Checkmate.

"Oh, this is funny," the beehive lady said after processing Vicki's card. "The balance for the December course in San Francisco is due today!"

With that, she handed me a printed invoice for the $320 remaining after Vicki's deposit. "Will that be cash or credit?"

"Death and taxes" I grumbled as I handed over my Visa.

"Thank you, sir," the beehive lady replied as she finalized the transaction. "You're going to love the Landmark Forum!"

I didn't love the Landmark Forum.

I didn't love the fact that the course took place in a room in which the blinds were drawn to outside stimulus, which in this case was San Francisco's lively Embarcadero. I didn't love the three consecutive 13-hour days—Friday, Saturday and Sunday.

Mostly, though, I didn't love the seminar leader, a hostile, middle-aged woman from Indianapolis who had none of the charm of the guy who oversaw Vicki's seminar in Cincinnati. She loudly berated the poor volunteers in the back of the room for offenses such as not having enough pens to go around or letting someone walk out of the room for a bathroom break during a group exercise. In the hallway during one of the early breaks, I overheard a group of gossipy gay men refer to her as "The Viper."

In all fairness, it was a most inopportune time to be rooting around my head—and certainly not in a hermetically sealed room. But the long weekend didn't pass without entertainment.

One of the exercises was to make a life-altering phone call, something that would patch a festering wound or right a longstanding wrong. We were advised to throw all caution to the wind. I racked my brain, but couldn't think of a single person whom I'd pruned from my life that I wanted to graft back into place. So I just hiked up Nob Hill in order to stir the oxygen tanks for the next long session of sitting. San Francisco is the best hill-walking city in the country, and I required a lot of tank-stirring that weekend.

When we were called back into session, there were some heartwarming results to report. One guy seemed hugely relieved after making plans to have an air-clearing meeting with his longtime business partner, with whom he'd developed an acrimonious and distrustful relationship. Another man had his first civil conversation in years with his ex-wife, who had full custody of the child that he longed to see. Over the course of the weekend, he kept us updated with more hopeful conversations with his ex.

In the three weeks between signing up for the seminar and attending it, one of my African-American neighbors tried to bet me that there wouldn't be a single black person at the seminar. "That's white folks' voodoo," he informed me. "Black people don't waste money on that shit."

I should have taken the bet. Of the 90 or so attendees, there was, in fact, a single black male—but he admitted that he was only there because a friend bribed him into accompanying her by paying his entire freight. While he was there, he apparently was intent on seizing the opportunity. He was the last of about a dozen volunteers who paraded to the microphone to report the results of the life-altering phone call assignment.

"Is everybody feeling alright?" he asked, as if he were introducing the band. He was clearly nervous, and clearly over-compensating for it. The Viper reassured him that he was in a no-judgment zone.

"So, um, my wife and I have been having our issues, like everyone else," he reported. "She was the first one I thought of when we were told to make our fearless phone call."

From my vantage point in the next-to-last row, I could see a few of the women in front of me getting misty in anticipation of the tale of romantic contrition that we all thought was forthcoming.

"Anyway, we got to talking," he said, "and I finally told her that I'm leaving."

Although we were in a no-judgment zone, I felt as though a standing ovation (especially a one-man standing ovation) would have cast me in an ill light with my fellow attendees. I'm not opposed to love in any form, but I admired the zealousness with which he attacked the task while I was rationalizing my way out of it.

On our next break, I found him sitting alone, so I introduced myself and congratulated him for his chutzpah. It seemed to cheer him up after the deafening silence that followed his announcement. Ten hours later, when we finally were released for the night, he looked like a man with some serious regrets about his daring dialing.

But the weirdest exercise of the long weekend, by far, was one in which we were supposed to keep our eyes shut while The Viper, who had no gift for storytelling, took nearly an hour to build a narrative. It started with us imagining that everyone in the room hated us. Once we had our heads around that, we were supposed to elevate our unpopularity to include everyone in San Francisco. Then we were directed to expand our paranoia to include the entirety of California, and so on, until we were the most maligned being on the planet.

One lady began crying early in the exercise. She was joined, in short order, by several sisters-in-wailing. Good lord, I thought. If the object was to make women cry, I should be leading the seminar.

Taking a page from the armed forces, that deconstruction of our morale was followed by a quick reversal in strategy. We were subsequently directed to imagine that we were universally loved; at first within the room and, by and by, around the world. As she clumsily boosted our popularity, The Viper began to laugh, a cold, creepy cackle that grew and grew, like the Grinch's heart on Mount Crumpit.

I had long since abandoned the exercise to mentally undress two of my female classmates, but even that was made untenable by the head-rattling decibel level of the Viper's chortling. I opened my eyes and glanced over at Paul, a financial industry whiz-kid with whom I'd bonded over the long weekend. The look on his face was priceless, an expression of horrified amusement. I glanced over my shoulder at Mai-Ling, a beautifully amusing woman with whom Paul and I had shared a few laughs during the grueling sessions. She was biting her lip in a painful attempt not to laugh out loud.

When the exercise ended with everyone in the room in complete bewilderment over the purpose of the past 60 minutes, the Viper's convoluted explanation seemed to be that life could sometimes be a cosmic joke, or a big cosmic joke with a haunting laughtrack, so don't sweat what others think of you. Or what you think others think. Landmark was big on "your interpretation of events in your life is merely your interpretation" exercises.

Until that point, I had tried to remain open to the possibilities of the weekend, but that bit of weirdness knocked me off the fence. Landmark wasn't my cup of tea. But in Landmark-speak, my interpretation of the weekend was merely my interpretation of the weekend.

But I'll happily debunk the cult myth. Cults are animals of prey, isolating the vulnerable from the herd. Although Landmark's sales pitches were relentless, their recruiters were no more exclusionary than the average car salesman.

I decided then and there that the Landmark Forum would be my last attempt at organized introspection. My first attempt, Catholicism, hadn't fared much better.

But all paths lead somewhere. It was during the dinner break on the final day of the seminar that I conspired with Paul and Mai-Ling, both of whom were a generation younger than me, to facilitate a means by which we could all keep in touch—all of us having rejected Landmark's vehicle for keeping in touch, which was to sign up for more courses. Thus was born the Circle of Trust & Beer Hiking Club.

19

The Circle Is Drawn

Some of the most prized real estate in Southern California is located along the Pacific Coast Highway. But in the Bay Area—where it is known as Highway 1—the coastal route is, with few exceptions, a ghostly populated, two-lane passage.

Heading north from fog-centric Montara Mountain, Highway 1 ducks inland at Pacifica. In the interest of contiguousness, it merges with other thoroughfares, but in essence is non-existent through San Francisco and across the Golden Gate into southern Marin County.

Highway 1 resumes its coastal identity at Muir Beach, population 310: roughly one hearty resident for each day of the year the unincorporated town is visited by fog.

Many tourists tend to think of California beaches in terms of the sunny, volleyball-friendly stretches of oceanfront in San Diego, Los Angeles, Orange and Ventura counties. Those with such preconceptions are often disappointed by blustery Muir Beach and other sandy destinations in Northern California. But redwoods and bikinis rarely thrive simultaneously, so we in the Bay Area make do with primitive rather than prurient pleasures. With our claims variously staked, we avoid civil unrest with our brethren in Southern California.

Compared to nearby Stinson Beach—where majestic Mount Tamalpais spills into the Pacific among an outbreak of cafes, restaurants, surf shops and cheesy lodgings—Muir Beach seems almost entirely uninterested in capitalism. The lone retail business is the Pelican Inn, a whitewashed, ivy-strewn Tudor lodging house with a tiny pub just off the lobby. Because the pub is invariably ass-to-elbow with clientele, much of the beer poured at the Pelican Inn is consumed on the inn's gorgeously manicured lawn.

After the fog burns off, a cold beer on the lawn of the Pelican Inn might be the premier après-hiking experience in all of California. That, paired with the awe-inspiring beauty of the trails above the town, made Muir Beach the logical jumping-off spot for the Circle of Trust & Beer.

It was there that we first gathered in February 2012, six weeks after our internment at the Landmark Forum. There were but six of us. It was all the same to me. I had been exploring California trails for well over a decade, the preponderance of them on my own. It suited my nature to be able to follow an intriguing trail when the whim struck, without regard to someone else's schedule or fitness level. It was by wandering countless mountains that I became familiar enough with them to guide others.

So I entered The Circle of Trust & Beer venture unencumbered by expectations. If others showed up, great. If not, I still got to hike. My zen approach probably would have met the approval of the Buddhist monks who oversaw Green Gulch Farm, separated by a few hundred yards of marshy trail from the Pelican Inn. I like to think that the town's namesake, John Muir, would have approved, as well.

There was an immediate sign that I might be tackling an uphill venture. Midway up the first ascent—just five minutes into our hike—Mai-Ling's husband, who was hung over, christened The Circle with an impressive and sustained bout of projectile vomiting.

Our small group recovered and fell into the natural rhythm of the hike, which duly rewards each challenging climb with a breathtaking vista. On a series of switchbacks on the leeward side of the hike, Mai-Ling launched into a tale of a recent excursion into San Francisco. After booking what she thought was going to be a spa day with the girls, she arrived to profound disappointment; the place was a gay bathhouse.

Feeling a bit silly that she didn't put "San Francisco" and "spa" together to form a logical conclusion, Mai-Ling convinced her girlfriends to roll with the punches. They disrobed and jumped into their hot tub. But while they were splashing around, one of them swallowed a mouthful of water and reported that the sodium level was freakishly high. Their discussion soon turned to speculation of the ingredients of the funky soup in which they were marinating.

In deference to the colorfully robed monks who occupy Green Gulch and the retreaters who flock to its Zen center on weekends, we tried to reel in the laughter as we alighted from the mountain. Green Gulch's Zen center, gardens, organic farm and horse pasture comprise what I have found to be the most glorious final mile of any hike in California.

With her tone subdued to reflect the surroundings,

the happy-go-lucky Mai-Ling closed her story with a confession. The oddest part of the day, she admitted, was "feeling invisible."

"What do you mean?" I asked.

"I was completely naked, and all those men were just looking right through me," she said. "I mean, in the gym, even straight women check each other out. But there I was, without a shred of clothing, and there wasn't a flicker of recognition in any of those guys' eyes."

What Mai-Ling didn't have to mention was that she was a head-turner of the highest order, clothed or not, and that few straight men had ever mistaken her for spa décor. And since she was significantly less ego-engulfed about her looks than many women with half of her fortune in that department, her pain was palpable.

"So it was the opposite of being objectified?" I inquired.

"Totally," she replied. "I was subjectified."

I understood all too well. We all want a human connection. Once I got my head around that basic tenet of existence, years after the fear-based fog of Catholicism had dissipated, it was easy to get past the ingrained homophobia of my youth. Nobody wanted to be subjectified.

But I was still crystallizing that thought when another member of our party suggested that heterosexual men could be conditioned to replicate the response of the gay men in the spa: "You just marry them!" she said.

As we ducked into the Pelican Inn, Mai-Ling made a motion that the most appropriate conversations for the Circle of Trust & Beer should be those that were entirely inappropriate for the workplace. There was nary a dissenting vote.

The Circle had been inaugurated.

But neither Mai-Ling nor her husband, who found little enjoyment in the day until quaffing back some hair of the dog, returned. For the next six months, The Circle limped along, fishing from a stagnant pool of Landmark refugees. Fortunately, we stayed true to the path she had proposed: the conversations were warped. Which is to say that they were honest.

Guided by the zen-acity and Muir-ism on which the Circle was founded, I was unfazed by the lack of growth ... for a while. I was putting a lot of effort into organizing Circle of Trust & Beer get-togethers, plotting the routes and describing them in detail via email, lest anybody commit over their head and there were any cardiac surprises on the trail. By and by, my enlightenment faded and I grew frustrated with the lack of return on my sweat equity.

There was one spike in attendance, five months after our founding, when next we returned to Muir Beach. The occasion was my 50th birthday. My ex-girlfriend and close friend, Sue, organized a bodacious day of hiking and hoisting. Scott Davis, my buddy from DePaul, flew in from Denver for the festivities. Traveling with Scott was another good friend from college, Roger, a fellow Ohioan and my brother in devotion to the Cincinnati Reds.

But where hiking was concerned, I intended to use the occasion to clear up some bad karma with Roger.

A few years earlier, Scott and I plotted out a summer hike in Death Valley, something so abjectly stupid that a ranger that I called to help with the details laughed for nearly a full minute—then told me he'd arrest us if we followed through. Unfazed, we locked down a date: July 10, based purely on the fact that the hottest temperature in recorded history had occurred on that date, in Death Valley, some seven decades prior. We figured that as long as we were going to risk life and/or a mark on our permanent record, we might as well experience once-in-a-lifetime temperatures. We compared notes and determined that the highest temperature we'd both experienced was identical: 122 Fahrenheit, by coincidence in Phoenix in different years. So "123 degrees or bust" became our mantra for the hike.

Our twisted plan worked like a charm. The digital temperature board on the Death Valley Post Office in the town of Furnace Creek on July 10 of that year displayed a high that was rare even in Death Valley— 130 degrees. But we weren't there to see it. Roger had begged onto the trip in the 11th hour, but the minutia of his nasty divorce nixed a July 10 rendezvous. For his sake, we postponed the trip two weeks, to July 24, when the thermometer climbed to a mere 119 degrees. Scott and I sulked through the hike as if we'd been banished to Siberia.

Still, the trip provided a memory for the ages. After a warm-up hike near Furnace Creek, we drove to the day's main event: Ubehebe Crater. Formed by an explosion of magma, the floor of the crater is lined by a rocky alluvial fan, which vents steam from the hydrovolcanic activity ever at work just below the surface. It's essentially a gateway to hell. I was wearing one of those all-purpose training watches, which measured heartbeat and calories and such, but it also had a temperature gauge. When I stuck my arm over the pit of the crater, the temperature reading soared from 119 to 138 degrees – and the alluvial fan through

A GOOD LOOK BEFORE DARK

which all the heat was being generating was still 500 feet below. On the surface where we stood, scalding air poured up and over the rim in near-gale force. It was as if someone had run the Santa Ana winds that blow through Southern California through a microwave.

It was under these conditions that Roger, perched precariously close to the crater's rim, had unzipped himself to pee. A compact man, he was lower to the ground than most. We'd all been chain-chugging water that day, and Roger's dam was bursting. When he unleashed the torrent, the broiling winds of Ubehebe took over, forging the stream into a boomerang that made its way directly into Roger's mouth. While Scott and I were futilely scrambling for our cameras, Roger turned to face the opposite direction in mid-piss, but simply wandered into another vector of winds in doing so, diverting the urine from his mouth into his eyes. Trying another angle, he was finally able to lower the return fire—onto his chest. Scott and I were on the ground by that point, not only because we were seizing with laughter, but also because the ground seemed to be the only place where the urine stream was unlikely to land.

Roger was acting pissy on my 50th birthday, as well. On the way home from picking up my friends at the San Francisco airport the night before, we bought a 12-pack, that, I figured, would last the weekend. After all, it was midnight before we got back to my place, and my plan was to have a quick toast with old friends and then hit the sack in preparation of the next morning's hike and the ensuing festivities (the Pelican Inn party was the first of two that day—Sue arranged another one in Alameda, where my East Bay friends who didn't like crossing bridges would gather at a bayside restaurant).

We twisted the lid on three beers, and hoisted one to the years. Then I went to bed. Scott hung out with

Roger and had one more beer, then plopped down on the couch to crash. When I roused them the next morning to get ready for the hike, the entire 12-pack was arrayed in my recycling bin. Roger had downed nine of them. He was heroically hung over the next day, and his grousing didn't stop until my good friend Linda took pity on me and ushered him away from the Muir Beach gathering to a tequila bar in Berkeley. By the time they arrived at the follow-up party in Alameda— two hours late—Roger was his old self.

Back in Muir Beach, the Circle grew as non-hiking friends joined the hill-hoppers on the sun-soaked lawn at the Pelican Inn. The pitchers seemed to magically appear from inside of the pub, and I merrily endured an afternoon of roasting from old friends and new. The general theme seemed to be that a meager wager in the 1980s that I'd live to see this day would have paid off like Microsoft stock.

The perfect storm of that afternoon—great hills, hops and humans—got me to thinking that such occasions need not be reserved for the milestones of life's trail. That's when somebody mentioned that I might better harvest the fruits of my labor if I put The Circle of Trust & Beer on Meetup.com.

I knew vaguely of Meetup, but had a preconceived notion that it was a forum for hooking up. I was mostly wrong, as has invariably been the case when I preconceived of anything. Meetup's target audience is unquestionably singles, but the idea is to pull people away from their laptops to participate in real-life activities, be it hiking, crocheting, bowling, bungee jumping from bridges or just playing bridge. There were some strange ones, to be sure, like the naked life-coaching group in suburban Phoenix or the alien-abduction support group in Southern California's San Fernando Valley.

After just three people showed up for my next hike in August, I decided that it was time to go the Meetup route. I paid my first quarter's dues, secured a catchy URL (*meetup.com/beerhike*) and opened the Circle of Trust & Beer (v. 2.0) for business in September 2012.

The dividends were immediate. In the three weeks between launch and the first hike, 80 people registered for the group and two dozen signed up for the first hike—which, naturally enough, was scheduled for Muir Beach. I figured if I couldn't hook them on hiking at that venue, they were lost causes.

On the day of the club's grand re-opening, 18 freshly minted Trustees showed up. That was triple the average attendance of the previous Circle excursions.

The only person with whom I'd had any previous contact was Lloyd. We were the same age and lived practically across the street from each other in the sleepy end of Alameda. It being California and all, Lloyd and I had no idea that the other existed until we met a few weeks earlier at the wedding of some mutual friends—450 miles to the south in Manhattan Beach.

Among the other attendees was Stephanie, an attractive blonde of German ancestry who taught at an elite Jewish school. Every hike with Stephanie was a recap of her failed dating ventures. She drilled me for a male's perspective on every one of them, which was akin to asking an arsonist about candle arrangements.

Of the 18 hikers that accompanied me on the Circle of Trust & Beer re-launch, half were never to be heard from again. Five became regulars. Four returned intermittently.

And I fell in love with one.

20

The Garden of Earthly Delights

When joining The Circle of Trust & Beer, the protocol is to answer a few questions designed by me and attach a picture. Most people went with the theme of the club and submitted a picture of themselves hiking or drinking beer, or both.

Kailia was doing neither. The photo was cropped at her chest and showed her adorned in a spaghetti strap scoop-top shirt, standing by a lagoon.

Her highlighted, shoulder-length brunette hair was tucked behind her right ear but dropped freely on the left, framing a round face bejeweled with almond eyes and made approachable by apple cheeks. Her ample lips and wide mouth showcased perfect—and perfectly polished—teeth. Her look wasn't exactly exotic, but the Syrian genes from the paternal side of her family hauntingly accentuated the Irish features she inherited from her mother.

Setting off the whole package were two tendrils of hair, one falling across her left eye and the other lodging in the corner of her mouth.

I was grounded enough in experience, however, to know that it was probably an illusion. The picture, I was sure, caught a moment in time where the whims of sun and shadow and wind, never to be repeated in such random combination, conspired to frame this woman as a goddess … with the possible aid of Photoshop.

The photo, as it turned out, was years old. But I didn't discover that for months, for she could easily pass as a decade younger and, when she wore her hair down with glasses instead of contacts—which was the case on our first meeting, the difference between her biological age and appearance was often even wider. I had some of her genetic gifts—most people erred on my age by 6 or 7 years, but that was wholly attributable to my immaturity. Somewhere in an attic a portrait of Kailia was aging rapidly, but the flesh-and-blood version was a sight to behold. Kailia later claimed that I did a double-take as she passed by while I was lacing my hiking boots on the tailgate of my Element.

We literally formed a circle and I gave a short intro address, after which we commenced another exercise that became integrally branded to the club: an introduction from everyone in attendance. In order to fast track the bonding process, I encouraged everyone to bullet-point the stops along their journeys to this place. As in, "Hi, I'm Sarah, originally from Buffalo, but I went to school in Austin and moved here from San Diego about a year ago." This being California, natives were few and far between, and the itinerant lists facilitated a lot of "hey, I spent some time in Chicago or Tampa, etc." conversations. Which was the whole idea.

Kailia, I learned in her intro, was from Boston but had lived in the Bay Area since shortly after college.

Off we marched into the haunting fog of Muir Beach and a new day for The Circle of Trust & Beer. I was thrilled with the turnout.

Kailia had not come alone. I may have very well done a double-take at her first glance, as she contended, but I definitely looked twice when the vehicle in which she arrived pulled up: an orange Honda Element with black trim—a duplicate of my ride. Elements, perfect toaster-boxers on wheels, were big among the outdoor and dog crowds in California because they could literally be hosed out, and thus were largely impervious to trail filth, animal hair, etc. Trouble was, they didn't sell very well anywhere else, and Honda discontinued them in 2011, the year after I bought mine.

When Kailia's chauffeur, whose name was Kram, alighted from the vehicle, we exchanged a brothers-in-Element handshake. Thus did I unwittingly establish an instant connection with Kailia—whom I saw (twice, apparently) just moments later.

Kram and I hit it off on the trail—in fact, we got along considerably better than he and Kailia. I came to find out they had dated a decade earlier. They bickered as if they had never made the transition to a platonic relationship, however. They reminded me of younger versions of my parents.

Kailia, however, was in mourning from a much fresher relationship that went south. I was in mourning for other reasons. But I did not mourn on the trails, steadfastly imploring John Muir's advice to "wash my spirit clean."

With the reformed group in its infancy, I had not yet developed a stable of pace-setters or sweepers. There was no need for such sophistication in the previous months and years, when I could generally count the members of my group on one hand. So that day, it fell to me to keep the head and tail of the group within frame.

It was a skill I developed rapidly and by necessity. On that inaugural hike, as I raced from mid-pack to the front of the group to direct The Circle through an ambiguous turn where the trail approached Highway 1, the two women lagging at the back of the group headed off in the wrong direction, toward a dangerous stretch of shoulder-less highway on which no pedestrian was meant to set foot. After rounding up the group and confirming that we were two shy of a full crew, I dropped my backpack and sprinted back toward the turn, finding them just as they were approaching a transitional mound that would have deposited them into traffic.

Toward the end of the hike, as we strolled through the Green Gulch Zen Center, I veered into the Garden of Earthly Delights with Stephanie and Kailia. The garden is one of my favorite spots on the planet. In the hypothetical "what if's?" that make up a life, I had long thought it would be an ideal place to get married (accompanied by the heavenly voice of the Cowboy Junkies' lead singer, Margo Timmons, of course).

Kailia and I stopped in front of the Bench of Temporary Reconciliation, a name I had given to the southwestern of the four diagonally positioned benches arrayed at each corner of the garden. Years earlier, on a hike with an ex-girlfriend, we stopped at the bench to clear the air about "unrighted wrongs" (her words) in our bygone relationship. I thought of it merely as burying the hatchet. In any case, nothing got righted and nothing got buried, because we ended up making out and temporarily reunifying, a bad idea all around.

Although I had learned decades earlier that talking to women about former girlfriends was a great strategy for abstinence, I told Kailia the story on the day we met because I thought she needed a laugh. It served its intended purpose. I pulled out my cell phone; in the metamorphosis of the Circle of Trust & Beer, we were now in dire need of photos for the website. I caught her smiling demurely in front of the Bench of Temporary Reconciliation. She looked like an angel. I fell in love with that photo.

Stephanie was lingering on the outside of the garden, pretending to be interested in the white roses, and taking all of this in. In the months that followed, she liked to say that she played witness to the fire's first spark.

The day didn't end without a hitch. The Pelican Inn, our planned post-hike watering hole, was closed for a wedding. Out came the phones. We came to a consensus on the Marin Brewing Company, 20 minutes away in the town of Larkspur, across the street from Marin County's largest ferry launch and just over the hill from the state's most notorious prison, San Quentin.

A good time was had by all, and the Circle of Trust got to keep its "& Beer" designation.

21

The Marriage Poll

K ailia answered my group email thanking everyone and giving them the details of the next hike, three weeks hence on Mount Tamalpais. She noted that she really enjoyed herself and was eager to hit more trails, so I invited her on a solo hike I had planned for that weekend. She didn't take the bait, so I let it go at that. I'd told her I hoped to see her on the next group hike.

I really didn't want to be that guy who fished for women out of his own Meetup group, one of the reasons I had been reticent about putting the group online in the first place. But she initiated contact again the next week, and we established a nice rapport by email and phone before the Mt. Tam excursion. A few days before the hike, I asked her to dinner on the night after the hike.

"As friends," she said.

"Of course," I said, lying in the manner of a billion men before me. I wondered, once again, why men and women felt compelled to play such games.

And I played it fairly straight all the way through dinner. But as I walked her to her car, I pulled her close and kissed her. She pulled away with the reluctance I had feared, but then laid her forehead against mine, inviting a repeat.

Way leads on to way, as Robert Frost said, and, with my 50th birthday astern, I stumbled into love again.

I vowed that I would go reluctantly, if at all. Trained as a journalist, I honed my skills in various newsrooms and approached life with a reporter's audacity. In my early 20s, I began taking an informal census that I came to call "The Marriage Poll."

As the poll's lone employee, and an unpaid one at that, I enthusiastically piled up the interviews. My M.O. became the stuff of legend among my friends. After spying a wedding ring in a bar, dinner party, gym, cab stand, concert—few venues were off-limits—I'd switch on the charm, exploit my credentials and commence the probe: "I've always had a professional curiosity surrounding the institution of marriage. Do you mind if I ask a few questions?"

The refusals were few and far between, from women or men. If the Marriage Poll was glib and shameless, it also was rooted in genuine fascination for the subject matter. Although I wrote nothing down, I arranged the information into cerebral categories with the diligence and emotional detachment of a deadline writer.

The Marriage Poll's stats mounted by the dozens, then by the hundreds, even after I abandoned journalism. As the years rolled on, I could fairly accurately predict the outcome of each inquisition as it was unraveling.

I unapologetically recited the poll's wildly

unofficial findings to anyone who asked, even as I continued to stockpile data. Some 85 percent of marriages, I estimated, were entered into for all the wrong reasons: infatuation; lack of alternatives; lack of experience with relationships; family pressure; ambition that failed to rise above a modicum of comfort with a partner; or simply throwing in the towel and settling after a certain age.

Thus, I concluded, were all those unions doomed to some sort of failure, be it divorce or indifference. The 15% that had a chance, I reasoned, still had to navigate a minefield of limitless perils—boredom, weight gain, ungrateful offspring, disease and death.

Marriage was a fool's bet. And love was its agent provocateur.

Then I met Kailia. On paper, we were a train wreck awaiting its cue. Kailia earned a master's degree so that she could teach autistic kids. I staged a fake college graduation so that I could fast-track a career consisting of writing about football and scarfing press-box hotdogs. She had never had a one-night stand. My résumé was littered with younger women and one-off encounters.

But we clicked. We connected on an intellectual level. Our warped senses of humor jibed. We laughed, loudly and often. We spent breathless hours hiking trails and together cherished countless Pacific sunsets from a myriad of postcard vantages. We slow-danced in her living room. I drew her out of her mourning period for the guy who came before me. She drew me out of a torpor of death.

Over the next year, I guided The Circle of Trust & Beer over dozens of trails in seven Bay Area counties, as well as an annual out-of-town hike in Yosemite National Park.

We took awe in the arrow-straight coastal redwoods of Mount Tamalpais, north of the Golden Gate Bridge, and the canyons of Douglas Firs from an overlook at Purisma Creek near Half Moon Bay, where we celebrated at a brewery overlooking the waters that hosted one of the world's gnarliest surfing contest, Mavericks. We sweated the steep grades and the crowds of Mission Peak in Fremont, and basked in the solitude of Butano State Park, virtually unchanged for a century. We stood in awe around a 1,200-year-old sequoia in Portola Redwoods State Park and counted deer by the dozens in the hills above Stanford University.

We grinded through the steep and sticky canyons of Mount Diablo, where I spotted my father's look-alike a few years earlier. We shared the mountain fables of the Miwok and Ohlone tribes who came before us, and celebrated the spirit of John Muir, the Scottish-American explorer and author, a century gone. We humped through the heat of the El Cerro climb in Sunol Regional Wilderness and danced in the rare, rare rains of California's great drought, sliding on the muddy slopes of Barnabe Peak, named after a donkey.

Twice a year, we hiked an urban route, up and down the steep, postcard-perfect streets of San Francisco. There in the fog that frequently engulfs the Eucalyptus trees that have commandeered the Presidio, a decommissioned military base that serves as the run-up to the Golden Gate Bridge, we dropped our backpacks and noshed on sandwiches, almonds, sliced avocados, chips and M&Ms (with peanuts!) as the gulls put on a chaotic aerobatic circus.

But The Circle of Trust & Beer returned to Muir Beach, our point of creation, again and again. Muir Beach came to define us, serving as our asylum, a familiar and familial place where our warped group could be replenished by all that we held sacred: the dirt trails, the crashing waves, the hidden beaches.

When we returned to Muir Beach, in March 2013, The Circle had swelled to over 400 members. As the group slipped out of the Garden of Earthly Delights, I grabbed Kailia's hand and guided her through the rose-covered trellis. We kissed deeply at the Bench of Temporary Reconciliation.

It was long about this time that growing pains were forcing me to make some decisions about the direction of the club. Kailia had been lobbying me for easier hikes; as a rule, the Circle of Trust & Beer didn't bother with any route that didn't have at least 1,200 feet of vertical ascent, but 1,700 feet was more the norm. I was happy to go on less ambitious hikes with Kailia as a twosome, but she enjoyed the group dynamic so much that she wanted me to tool The Circle to her specifications. I invariably changed the subject whenever she broached it, but may have agreed to re-examine the issue once or twice under the duress of her exquisite physical assets.

Kailia wasn't the only one waging a campaign. Three months after Kailia and I met, Laura joined the Circle and, one hike later, Tim did the same. They were a generation younger than me and emerging from divorces. "What about some harder hikes?" Laura asked over a pint at the Marin Brewing Company as she plopped down in the seat to my left, a tradition that would continue for the next year-and-a-half, until she moved out of the Bay Area. As a result, she was bestowed with the nickname "Left Wing."

Tim, tall and angular with glasses, showed up at every hike in a Ferrari hat, a company for which he was a lead mechanic. Tim was from Iowa and measured his words, but was considerably more liberal with a smile. A brilliant mind under the hood of a car, Tim let his motor run idle on the weekends and I spent a lot of time sharing the trails with him when I needed to decompress from my organizer duties. So when he doubled down on Laura's request, I took the matter to heart.

"Just think about, it Brian," Tim said, his voice rising to the level of an accountant reviewing a modest debit, as vociferous as Tim seemed to get on any particular subject. "It seems like there are a lot of grinders in this club who would gladly tackle the tougher peaks."

They were right. Twice in the previous three years, I had risen to the challenge of Yosemite National Park's Half Dome, California's signature day hike with nearly 5,000 feet of altitude gain over 8.5 miles and a death-defying cable climb up a seemingly vertical granite face to finish. Tim and Laura were keenly aware of Kailia's feedback and were determined that the persona of The Circle of Trust & Beer Hiking Club would be shaped in the image of its founder rather than his girlfriend.

Laura, a management-level buyer for a national fashion merchandiser, was an effervescent soul, wise beyond her 28 years. On a hike above the secluded beach town of Stinson Beach, I once offered anyone $20 for a picture capturing Laura *not* smiling. I kept my cash. Pretty in the most unassuming of ways, like a curvy film star of the 1950s sans the makeup, she quickly found her way into my heart in the manner of a little sister. Or daughter, since on the one occasion I met her father, we discovered that we had graduated high school the same year.

Laura's father had ridden cross-country from Minnesota on a Harley and joined us on a hike. As we conversed around the fire pit at the oceanside Half

Moon Bay Brewery, Laura's father and I excused ourselves and went to the bar to finish our drinks when we discovered that the pit wasn't the sole source of sparks from our little roundtable discussion. Laura and Tim were clearly connecting. On that very night they would share their first kiss. Eighteen months later, they would say good-bye to their careers and move to her Minnesota hometown. In early 2015, they married. The Circle of Trust & Beer added a matrimony to its résumé.

Long before they departed for the Snow Belt, however, I absorbed their counsel.

I sincerely hoped that my relationship with Kailia did not fade away. But the sheer volume of evidence in my past made that a longshot bet. The safe money was that I would, at some point, throw a wrench into the works. In the meantime, I could either heed Kailia's remarkably consistent pleas to tone down my hikes, or I could listen to the grinders, who were merely reinforcing what my heart was telling me. The object, as far as I was concerned, was to avoid the worse-case scenario, which would have been losing Kailia *and* finding myself herding a bunch of Sunday dog-walkers over relative molehills a year or two down the line.

Thus was formed, in 2013, The Semi-Circle of Trust & Beer, in which our motto became "Higher. Harder. Faster." If nothing else, we would remain sophomoric to the end.

The Semi-Circle was poorly named, reinforcing the theory that charters should not be written on bar napkins. Had I known how many hundreds of times I would be asked to explain its meaning over the next few years, I surely would have gone with something like "Full Circle" or "The Ring of Fire" to make it a little more obvious that hikes thusly named would tackle steeper inclines and longer trails.

"Semi-Circle" was meant to sound semi-exclusionary, like a subset, which it was, since no first-timers were permitted to tackle Semi-Circle hikes. You had to attend at least one regular Circle of Trust & Beer hike to get to know the culture of the club as well as get a sense for where our thermostat was set on the physicality level. The breathless ascensions of the Semi-Circle were poor venues for introductions.

Kailia, understandably, was a bit taken aback when I told her that I not only had decided against the junior varsity version of hiking that she had pinned her hopes upon, but would, in fact, be making tracks toward the opposite pole. I promised Kailia that I would limit Semi-Circle hikes to once a month. She suggested that she would avail herself for intimate contact at similar intervals.

"Well," I replied, not even bothering to take off my shoe before inserting it in my mouth, "at least now you know which hikes *not* to go on."

Needless to say, I slept on the couch that night, alone with my mental maps of area trails that might qualify for my new Semi-Circle program. Mostly, though, I thought about Kailia's semi-nude body in the next room, and how I could possibly bridge the daunting Canyon of Assholes between us. I faded off in a fog of regret.

I awoke to the sound of running water. I shot off the couch and intercepted Kailia between the bathroom and her bedroom. I grabbed her hand and steered her into the middle of her living room. I clicked on my iPhone, put one bud from my headphones in her left ear and the other in my right. She fell into me as we slow-danced to Jimmy Buffett's "Come Monday,"

When we got to our favorite line, I sang along, softly, in her open ear: *"We can go hiking on Tuesday. With you I'd walk anywhere."*

We swayed, arm in arm, in the moonlight of her apartment overlooking the foothills of the Santa Cruz Mountains. The song was set to repeat mode, but I didn't dare tinker with the vibe of that perfect moment. I would have joyously endured "Come Monday" a hundred times. But Kailia fell asleep on her feet, in my arms.

I knew, then and there, that I was falling hard. Damn. No good could come of this.

22

The Circle Inflates

The Circle of Trust & Beer thrived. By the outset of 2013, the word was out. Although the Bay Area is rife with hiking clubs, few had our cache, with perfect hikes pulled from my mental catalog and growing relationships with breweries across the Bay Area. Our ranks swelled to 500 and, in 2014, past 1,000. We were well on our way to 1,500 at the end of 2015.

My write-ups of the hikes were essentially an online book, with stats on the mileage and vertical gain, some history and geology factoids. Most important, however, was the story of why I felt obliged to share the hike with The Circle. Each was, in a sense, a glimpse into my soul.

I felt deeply indebted to those who had walked and carved the trails before me, in particular, John Muir. The man credited as the founder of the national park system and the Sierra Club fought for the sustenance of the trails we walked a century after his death. I felt no small responsibility for keeping his spirit alive on every hike.

Passion begets passion, and soon the hikes were populated with seekers of all sorts. Membership expanded by the dozens, then the hundreds. Muir's quotes were some of the most inspirational in my life, but I rarely felt the need to recite them in The Circle of Trust & Beer. Human speech, I'd come to believe, wasn't necessarily the highest form of communication. Muir knew this well when he wrote that "the clearest way into the universe is through a forest wilderness." Preaching it only would have undermined the powerful revelation that each hiker experienced upon his/her arrival, in his/her own time, at Muir's sacred truth.

But let's give beer its due credit in the blossoming of The Circle of Trust & Beer Hiking Club. I quickly dismissed thoughts of competing with some of the Bay Area's largest hiking groups as the folly of ego. I knew I could host 50-60 hikers as well as any of the hiking groups that were letting all comers through the gate. But at what cost? Where the hell was I going to reserve post-hiking space for five or six dozen people at a craft brewery or brew-pub on a Saturday afternoon or evening? In the San Francisco Bay Area, no less?

I immediately dropped my limit down to 44 hikers, thinking it would be an easy number to manage. After just one such hike, however, I realized I was doing more herding than conversing. On the next hike, I lowered the max, once again, to 33 hikers. Eureka! I had found my sweet spot—a group in which I could nimbly (with a lot of hustling) keep track of the head and tail of the caterpillar, so to speak, and still secure a post-hike group reservation at the places that formed the backbone of the craft brewery movement in Northern California.

Therein lied the gap between The Circle of Trust & Beer and all other hiking clubs—we sealed our trail bonds by rewarding the effort. Thirty-three became as branded to the group as our noon hiking starts and our unambiguous motto: "Climb. Descend. Drink."

There were all kinds of statistics by which we could have measured our success: the physical growth of the club; the fact that hikes often filled within minutes of announcing them; and by the emails, texts and personal asides I received about the impact the group had made upon members' lives.

But to me, one metric dwarfed them all. At the outset of 2013, when we began to experience real growth, the average hang-out time at our post-hike brew gatherings was 90 minutes. A year later it was two hours. By mid-2015, it wasn't unusual for Trustees to linger for close to three hours. I found myself at the center of a universe of bonding.

Other than the Semi-Circle conundrum, it was remarkably smooth sailing from the outset. Before I posted on Meetup, I was lucky to draw a half-dozen hikers to my obsessively detailed excursions. In 2013, every hike was maxing out within minutes. By the end of that year, it wasn't uncommon for the wait list— what we came to call the "Velvet Rope"—to exceed the number of confirmed hikers.

I won't say I didn't take a free beer here or shot of bourbon there to part the Velvet Rope every now and then, but out-and-out graft wasn't my style. Truth be told, between the annual subscription fees for the website and the group food and beer tabs that sometimes came up short, I was losing money on The Circle of Trust & Beer.

But it was a loss-leader, as far as I was concerned, like the 2-for-1 cartons of soda stacked in front of a grocery store: it got people in the door to experience the gospel according to Muir. And because I didn't sweat it, the universe took care of such trivialities, by and by, there was abundance of cash in the till after all had chipped in, and Kailia and I sometimes drank for free.

Kailia did not share my love of the ascent. I caught her grumbling aloud near the back of the pack on one particularly challenging diagonal stretch among the redwoods at the top of the Oakland hills, pulled her aside and reminded her that she should be the last person undermining the spirit of the club. "Fine," she said, with an undertone of familiar defiance. Kailia liked to be in charge.

A day earlier, she told me about a particularly challenging student with whom she had been doing battle for the better part of a semester. They came to a truce when the student, who complained loudly about homework each day, agreed to keep on hating homework but vocalize another attitude. Thus had Kailia been greeted at the beginning of the school day for the previous week with the rambunctious mantra of "I love homework!" being bellowed from the back row.

A few hundred yards down the trail, as I pulled away from Kailia and crested the hill into a grove of brilliantly dappled redwoods, a shout from below echoed off the ridge.

"I love hills! I looooovve hills," Kailia shouted, pausing the entire group in its tracks.

I waited for her to catch up. I could see the Dr. Seuss smile on her face before she fully rounded the bend. I waited for the group to pass, grabbed her by the hand and pulled her behind a tree. "That's my girl," I said, kissing her, something we never did in plain sight on the trails.

When next we returned to Muir Beach, a thought came to me as I herded the group out of the Garden of

Earthly Delights for the final mile of trail back to the parking lot. I would put a ring on Kailia's finger, in this very place, by the end of the year.

I had better get busy.

That very night, I laid awake deep into the night, staring across San Francisco Bay from my bedroom on the island of Alameda. Kailia was breathing heavy in the nook of my right arm, the place in the universe where I hoped she felt most safe. My arm was numb and I desperately wanted to stretch my hike-cramped legs. But I wanted the moment to stretch on. Her breath synced with heartbeat, and I floated to a higher plane of existence. This was, I surmised, the apex of the human condition. It was as enlightening as it was jarring. Where in the hell was I supposed to go from here?

I turned to the prurient, a trail well-traveled. I pulled back the covers and looked her over, head to toe. She was achingly beautiful. She had fallen asleep in her robe, but I could still see her silken breasts softly rising with each breath. She subconsciously drew me tighter even as I pulled away to admire the entirety of her landscape. She kissed me softly, unaware of her actions. I was hopelessly in love, and the fight-or-flight instincts that accompanied that concession, I decided, were the bane of much of the misery on Planet Earth.

"I love you Kailia," I whispered into her ear, safe in the knowledge that she was still asleep.

I popped an Ambien in my mouth and rolled toward her to embrace sweet oblivion. I was nearing the netherworld that demarcates the first haze of sleep from profound thought when I was startled by a voice.

"Be careful what you wish for, Brian Patrick Higgins. I love you, too."

23

Westward Ho

*T*he fog tumbled down the western slope of Montara Mountain, spilling toward the ocean in a slow-motion avalanche.

I could scarcely make out the forms in front of me, but I knew they were numerous. For this particular hike, I had rolled back The Circle of Trust & Beer's limit of 33 and allowed the RSVPs to go unchecked. Until this day, I had led every one of the group's excursions. But I felt compelled to play the role of sweeper, for anyone who fell behind me would surely be lost in the swirling sea of precipitation engulfing this stretch of hills. The Fog Machine was turned up to full throttle.

As we rose above the marine layer, the group came into focus. I was stunned to see not dozens, but hundreds on the trail ahead.

As their forms became familiar, their stories reverberated through my head, like the fog swirling off the ridges. The countless divorces and the deaths they had endured. The injuries, physical and otherwise, they had overcome. I alone stood sentry over the catalog of pain in front of me, and the healing process they had undertaken when they joined this group.

We, The Circle of Trust & Beer, were one, rooted together in transcendence like redwoods, suckled by the fog.

As we neared the apex, the masses parted to allow me through. I met their eyes, each and all, as I surged ahead.

Somebody had rigged a makeshift platform over the fencing that surrounds the power station scarring Montara's summit. I leaped to climb the chain-link fence bordering the area, but caught my right hand on a rusty bolt and gashed it deeply. I lost my grip and fell back. A hundred hands absorbed me, and eased me up the fence to the plywood stage that had not existed an hour earlier.

My time had come.

The largest Circle ever gathered turned about as one, facing me. In the gloaming, I could hear a few sobs.

"First of all," I shouted, beginning my sermon on the mount, "there's no crying in The Circle. Every trail ends where it begins, and begins where it ends.

The whimpering subsided. From the back of the group, someone shouted. "Speak up you, you blustery Irish S.O.B.!" The tension, thankfully, was broken in a torrent of laughter.

I cleared my throat and ratcheted up the volume.

"John Muir advised us to 'Climb the mountains and get their good tidings' " I continued. "He also said, 'In every walk in nature one receives far more than he seeks.'

"It has been a century since Muir walked the trails that we have shared these many years. Quite quickly, a century will pass after the last of us walks among the redwoods that stand sentry over the generations. Drink deeply of your time here. I certainly did."

As the fog gave way to dusk, silence fell over The Circle. A coyote howled in the gathering darkness hundreds of feet below, answered by the distinctive "kee-eeeee-arr" of a red-tailed hawk as it descended in wide circles above prey unseen by other mountain beings.

"Amen, Brother Hawk," I shouted, my voice already cracking and growing hoarse with exertion and emotion.

"Amen!" came the remarkably unified chorus of hundreds.

"Kee-eeeee-arr" came the reply from above.

"I leave you with this, my fellow Trustees, from the lips of Albert Einstein: 'Our task must be to free ourselves by widening our circle of compassion to embrace all living creatures and the whole of nature and its beauty.'

"Thank you for walking these sacred temples with me these many years. Go with your gods, whoever they may be. Mine live among the trees and inhabit the slopes and summits."

Pausing on the exhalation, I heard my last few words echo back.

"I was prepared to say that I now turn The Circle over to you," I said, my voice straining with emotion. "But ...

"But ... I cannot proffer to you what has always been yours."

I reached into my backpack, which had been lightened considerably by the years in which I had become adept at stowing only what I needed, and no more. I pulled out the bottle of Triple Rock Pinnacle Ale I had stashed for the occasion. I unscrewed the top with my injured hand, relishing the pain of the cap's aluminum ridges as they dug further into the exposed meat and carved a new tributary of blood, which fell across my cheek as I held the bottle aloft.

I was surprised to see that hundreds of bottles had already been hoisted before me.

"Sláinte!" I toasted.

"Sláinte!" came the unified reply, boomeranging off the peak and reverberating through the canyon below.

As The Circle imbibed, the silence retreated like the coyote's prey, replaced first by murmuring, then staccato bursts of laughter, then wholesale cacophony.

I paused to sweep my gaze across their faces, one by one, for the final time. There was Kermit, raising a lighter. Stephanie raised her bottle and blew a kiss as she brushed her date's hand off her shoulder.

Vicki Commeans, teary-eyed, waved from mid-pack.

Scott Davis, my buddy from college, was working his way through the crowd toward me, but was diverted when he caught sight of my parents, who had surprised all of us by making the climb without so much as a word of rancor. Father Mike was interceding in one of their arguments. They had consumed three beers apiece, thanks to my brother Dennis, who was now reaping the rewards of an ascent encumbered by the 12-pack bursting the seams of his backpack.

At long last, I caught the doe eyes that had stopped me in my tracks on the first Circle of Trust & Beer hike. Kailia smiled knowingly and gave me a wink, and my heart jumped as it had that first day. She was still beautiful. From behind her in the throng, Kailia's husband leaned forward and kissed her cheek.

One-by-one, they turned to begin the slow descent, clicking on their flashlights and halogen headlamps as they passed me.

I remained in place until the procession of light, a half-mile in length, wound its way downward into the Fog Machine and re-emerged below, trickling out of sight in singularity.

"Caaaaaawwww" was the last thing I heard before the splat on my knee.

I was jolted back to the here-and-now by disbelief; I had been defecated upon by the overfed black crow which only moments earlier was scrounging among the remains of my half-eaten sandwich on Table Rock, 600 feet above Stinson Beach.

A GOOD LOOK BEFORE DARK

I did not know how long I had been mesmerized by the lights of the ship as it steamed its way north by northwest over the horizon, but a fading halo in the western sky was the only evidence that the sun had recently been afloat on the vast Pacific. I must have been lost in thought for the better part of an hour. The days were still desperately short as the new year emerged from the long shadows of the solstice on Mount Tamalpais.

I thought of Kailia, and wondered if perhaps a courtship with the man with whom she would finally settle was underway. I wished her well.

I thought of my parents, and was reassured by the odd warm winds wafting up from the beach that they had, at long last, found contentment.

I struggled to my feet, stiffly, and found some leaves to wipe the guano from my knee. I smiled widely at the impish universe.

Facing me was a hasty retreat downhill, for I had forgotten to pack a flashlight. I lifted my ponderous backpack and could not help but think that it must have been the only thing I could have possibly forgotten among the weighty clutter within.

I headed down, into the setting sun, following the trail of John Muir and my parents and everyone now departed. I would join them soon enough.

But not today. I had not yet come full circle.

BRIAN PATRICK HIGGINS

Acknowledgments

To the strong women who have guided me on this path:

To Kerri Abdinoor, who pointed the way.

To Linda Hinton, a maverick whose support from start to finish kept me going when my spirits flagged.

To the members of the Bay Area chapters of *Shut Up & Write*, a group that did exactly what its title purported. Many thanks to my early writing partners, Lisa Carrera and Bianca Gandolfo.

To Allyson Spence, for the bright light you shined upon my trail. May you keep bagging life's peaks.

To Monique Luttrell, for standing by the side of the trail bemused, waiting for me to figure it out.

To Jaime Thompson, an unimpeachable editor, friend and fellow Buckeye nut. O-H!

To Christine Caserta, for guiding me home.

To Vicki Commeans, for giving me a stage.

Special Thanks

To Jane Higgins, for instilling my love of the written word. See you in the Hereafter Lounge!

To Erin, Julie and Brandy Higgins, for holding our family together during the darkest hours.

To Debbie Bisaillon, who shepherds us on the trails and shepherded this book into form.

A Mountain of Gratitude

To my friend, fellow writer and impeccable editor, Claire Splan, without whom I'd still be wandering the wilderness. This book is as much yours as mine.

About the Author

Brian Patrick Higgins is a former sportswriter for the *Savannah Morning News*, *Phoenix Gazette*, *Fort Worth Star-Telegram* and *Oakland Tribune*. He has served on the board of directors of the *Football Writers Association of America*. His media training clients have included dozens of NFL players.

He's the founder of a band of weekend warriors—The Circle of Trust & Beer Hiking Club—which numbers more than 1,300 members. Wanna join us? See info below.

A native of Columbus, Ohio (and rabid Ohio State Buckeyes fan), Brian has been exploring and cataloging California trails since relocating from Texas in 1995. He lives in Alameda, an island city in San Francisco Bay.

Follow Brian

www.hillsandhops.com

Facebook: /brianpatrickhiggins & /hillsandhops

Instagram: #hillsandhops

The Circle of Trust & Beer Hiking Club:
meetup.com/beerhike

To organize a book tour stop or public speaking event:
tour@hillsandhops.com

Made in the USA
Charleston, SC
09 November 2015